UNSHACKLED

UNSHACKLED

Overcoming Debt, Poverty, and Self-Doubt to Build Wealth, Legacy, and Purpose

By

Stephen E. Kent

Copyright

For permission requests contact: info@stephenekent.com
Published by SEK Publishing

This book is intended for educational and inspirational purposes only. The author is not a licensed financial advisor. Readers should consult qualified professionals before making financial decisions.

Printed in the United States of America.

Dedication

1. GOD

For breathing life into my bones and trusting me with the assignment of fulfilling YOUR dreams for my life. I row. YOU steer. YOU opened doors I never knew existed and protected my path even when I didn't understand the detours. All for YOUR Glory.

2. My Dear Mama (Rest in Sweet Peace)

Your strength, sacrifice, and your 'Be the Best' mantra shaped the man I became. I AM because of you.

3. My Sons

You were my 'why' when money was tight and stress was high. Let this book be proof that discipline pays off and a reminder that you can go even farther.

4. The 95%

The ones who were told they would never make it. The ones who grew up PO, not poor. This book is your permission slip, your blueprint, your spark. Let's make millionaires ON PURPOSE.

Financial freedom is not reserved for the lucky.

It belongs to the disciplined.

Preface

I didn't grow up with wealth, connections, or a safety net. I grew up with a praying mother, a strong back, and a belief that life had to offer more than survival.

This book is the product of that belief and the hard, humbling, often painful lessons I learned on my journey toward becoming a self-made millionaire. If you're holding this book, you're not looking for hype. You're looking for hope and a real strategy. You want a roadmap. That's what this is: a blueprint built on discipline, tested through failure, and grounded in faith.

My millionaire journey isn't just about my climb. It's about your launch.

Acknowledgments

I didn't get here alone.

To Molly, thank you for your dedication and the sacrifices you made to help bring this book to life.

To Anna-Maija, thank you for believing in the vision and helping organize these ideas into a flow that serves readers.

And to my readers, thank you for trusting me with your time. May every page move you closer to freedom.

Table of Contents

The Journey

Brave, Beautiful and Resilient Mama and her four gallant sons! Being our best in every situation.

Shy Stephen (1st Grade)

Curious Stephen (4th Grade)

Confident Stephen (6th Grade)

The Journey Continues

Colonel Stephen E. Kent
Comptroller, United States Forces Korea

Kent
Korean Basketball League

Kent
Author / Founder BTBF

How to Use This Book

This book isn't meant to be rushed. It's meant to be applied.

Unshackled is part story, part strategy, and part financial playbook. Each chapter builds on the last, guiding you from financial struggle to financial freedom, step by step. But transformation doesn't come from reading. It comes from **action**. So, here's the best way to use this book.

Step 1: Read for Understanding

Your first read-through is about exposure. Learn the concepts. Understand the mindset shifts. See the full blueprint. Don't worry about mastering everything yet. Just absorb the journey.

Step 2: Highlight the Principles

When something jumps off the page, highlight it. Underline ideas that challenge your thinking. Mark systems you want to implement. Your copy of this book should become personal. Dog-eared pages.
Highlighted passages. Notes in the margins. Because this isn't just a book. It's a tool.

Step 3: Apply the ACTION Steps

At the end of the chapters, you'll see three sections:

CONSIDER – Questions that help you reflect
ACTION – Simple steps to implement immediately
DOABLE – A practical step you should do within 48 hours

These aren't suggestions. They're the bridge between knowledge and transformation. Do them.

Step 4: Build the Habit of Financial Discipline

Wealth isn't built through dramatic moments. It grows through small habits repeated consistently. Budgeting. Saving. Investing. Learning. One disciplined decision at a time. That's how ordinary people build extraordinary wealth.

Step 5: Teach What You Learn

The final chapters challenge you to pass this knowledge forward. Teach your children. Mentor young people. Share financial wisdom with friends and family. Because the real power of financial literacy is not just personal freedom. It's generational change.

A Final Thought Before You Begin

The strategies in this book are simple. But simple does not mean easy. They require patience. They require discipline. They require consistency. But if you commit to applying what you learn, something remarkable begins to happen. Momentum builds. Confidence grows. Options appear. And slowly, steadily, the chains that once held you back, begin to break. That's the journey you're about to begin. Welcome to the path. Welcome to the process. Welcome to the life... **Unshackled.**

A Promise to the Reader

If you read this book and apply the principles inside it, three things will change in your life: You will understand how money truly works. You will stop repeating the financial mistakes that trap most families for generations. And you will begin building a future defined by freedom instead of fear.

This book is not about getting rich quickly. It is about becoming financially unshackled. Let's begin.

Chapter 1: From "PO" to Paid: A Story of Struggle, Sacrifice, and Financial Freedom

We didn't grow up poor. We were *PO.* So PO we couldn't even afford the "-or." That meant food stamps, government cheese, shut-off notices, and hand-me-down clothes patched together by Mama's tired hands.

My father left my mother with four boys and never looked back. No visits. No child support. Just gone. Mama told her lawyer one thing: "Just give me my sons. I'll figure out the rest." And she did.

She raised four boys in the ghettos of Mississippi with nothing but grit, faith, and an unbreakable will. Bill collectors called our house like clockwork. I can still hear the tension in my mother's voice when she answered the phone, trying to sound calm while holding back fear. We learned early how to survive. How to stretch a dollar. How to hustle. How to pray.

My older brothers joined the Army straight out of high school. Not because they were chasing adventure, but because they wanted to help put food on the table. They carried the weight of our family before most teenagers were even thinking about responsibility.

Then one afternoon, everything changed.

The Moment That Changed My Life

I was mowing Mr. Dickey's yard. He had bought me a sweatshirt, and I was working to pay him back. Mr. Dickey was my algebra teacher at Jefferson High School. Later he became our principal, and eventually the county superintendent. But to me, he was something even more important. He was someone who believed in me.

After I finished mowing, he sat me down and said, "Your mama called. She wanted you to know Dean Johnson from Alcorn State stopped by. Based on your ACT scores, they're offering you a full academic scholarship. Tuition. Room. Board. Books. And a $225 stipend each semester." I couldn't believe it. I had just finished the 11th grade. But I hesitated.

I told him I was about to become captain of the basketball team. After two injury-filled seasons, I was finally healthy and ready to play. Mr. Dickey looked at me and asked one simple question that changed my life forever. "You going pro?" I lowered my head. "Probably not." He nodded and said, "Then go to college." So, I did.

Mama's Mantra

From that moment forward, I carried the weight of my family's sacrifices and my mother's belief in us. Mama had one rule she repeated constantly: **Be the best.** Be the best in school. Be the best in sports. Be the best in behavior. No excuses. Just excellence.

College felt like a dream. Classes every other day. Freedom. Friends. Dorm life. But there were dangers on campus too. Banks showed up offering credit cards to students who had never been taught how interest worked. I signed up for five. Many of my classmates used theirs heavily. We didn't understand debt because no one had ever taught us the rules of the money game. We grew up dodging bill collectors, not studying compound interest.

Still, I pushed forward. I graduated with honors, earned my commission as a United States Army officer, and left Mississippi determined to build something different. I sent money home. Bought Mama a car. Started building a life.

I served my country for twenty-five years, eventually serving as a Colonel, and retiring as the Chief Financial Officer (CFO) at the three-star level. I led soldiers, traveled the world, and managed multimillion-dollar budgets. From the outside, it looked like success. But here's the truth. Even with all of that success, we were still living paycheck to paycheck. Not because we had to. Because that was all we knew.

The Wake-Up Call

Eventually I realized something powerful: education does not automatically equal financial wisdom. You can have degrees. You can have promotions. You can even lead organizations and still not truly understand how money works. That realization forced me to change. I studied. I failed. I made expensive mistakes. But I kept learning.

Eventually I broke the cycle. I became Vice President of Finance and CFO at multiple colleges. I built financial freedom. I eliminated consumer debt. I created systems that finally worked. But none of it came easy. It came through discipline. Through humility. Through lessons that cost me time, money, and pride. That is why this book exists. Not to impress you, but to equip you.

Here's something most people are never told early enough. The majority of Americans will depend heavily on Social Security to survive in retirement. In other words, only a small percentage of people ever achieve true financial independence. Not because they lack intelligence. Because no one taught them how money actually works. No one handed them a blueprint.

That changes right now. This book will show you the traps I fell into and the systems that helped me climb out. I will show you what I did wrong and what finally worked. Because the truth is simple. It doesn't matter where you start. What matters is where you decide to go.

If a kid raised in the ghettos of Mississippi by a single mother can build wealth, so can you. But it takes more than hope. It takes a plan. A mindset. And the courage to break the cycle. Let's build something new together.

Your past may explain your starting point, but it does not get to decide your destination.

CONSIDER

Where did your financial mindset come from?

Our beliefs about money rarely appear on their own. They are shaped by parents, environments, and experiences we absorbed as children. Understanding where those beliefs came from is the first step toward changing them.

My mindset was shaped by watching my mother stretch every dollar while raising four boys alone. Her determination taught me resilience, but our household also showed me how easily financial stress can control a family's life.

Have you ever made a financial decision driven by fear or the desire to escape struggle?

Many money mistakes are not caused by bad math. They are caused by emotion. Fear, shame, pressure, and the desire to look successful can lead us into decisions that sabotage our future.

What childhood belief about money still affects your decisions today?

Some beliefs help us grow. Others quietly hold us back. When you identify the beliefs shaping your decisions, you gain the power to rewrite your financial story.

Today, information is everywhere. Books, libraries, mentors, and technology can teach you what previous generations never had the chance to learn. Once you begin learning and applying the right principles, something powerful happens. Confidence grows. Momentum builds. The story begins to change.

You stop surviving and start building.

ACTION

Document your financial origin story.

Write down what you observed growing up about money. What habits did the adults around you practice? What lessons were spoken, and what lessons were never discussed?

Identify the turning point you want to create.
Your past shaped your financial identity, but it does not control your future. Writing your story allows you to see where you started and where you want to go.

DOABLE

Write down one painful financial lesson from your life.

What happened? What did it teach you? What decision will you make differently going forward? Pain is often life's greatest teacher. When you capture the lesson, you transform the pain into wisdom.

Chapter 2: Unshackled Thinking: How Millionaires See the World Differently

The real shift from poverty to prosperity does not start in your paycheck. It starts in your perspective. Money is often the last thing to change. Long before wealth appears in your bank account, it must take root in your thinking. That means the most important financial work isn't external. It's internal. It's how you see the world, how you respond when things get difficult, and how you interpret your own potential.

For most of my life, I believed wealth belonged to other people. People born in better neighborhoods, people with powerful last names, people with connections I didn't have. But poverty is not only financial. It's often mental. Escaping it required me to confront the way I was thinking.

The Mindset Gap

Millionaires think differently. Not because they are better people, but because they trained their minds to look for possibility where others see limits. When something goes wrong, most people ask, *"Why does this always happen to me?"* Unshackled thinkers ask a different question: *"What's the opportunity here?"* That question alone can change the direction of a life. When a limited mindset sees a closed door, it walks away. An unshackled mind looks for a window. And if there's no window, it builds a new door.

Another difference is ownership. Millionaires do not wait for permission, and they do not expect life to be fair. Instead, they focus on what they can control. They take ownership of their decisions, ownership of their habits, and ownership of their future. That ownership builds wealth one decision at a time.

The Ownership Principle

Most people ask, *"Can I afford this?"* Unshackled thinkers ask a different question: *"What return will this produce?"* That shift from cost thinking to return thinking changes everything. It changes how you evaluate time, money, relationships, and energy. It's no longer just about what something costs. It's about what it produces.

At one point in my life, I caught myself saying something dangerous: *"I will never have enough."* That sentence carried more power than I realized. So, I changed it. Now I say, *"I am learning how to manage more."* Language matters. The words you repeat become the beliefs you accept, and the beliefs you accept become the behaviors you live. When your language improves, your decisions begin to improve with it.

Builders vs. Consumers

Unshackled thinkers also understand the difference between building and consuming. They do not try to prove their worth through spending. Instead, they focus on building things that last longer than they do. Assets. Ideas. Businesses. Impact. Consumption may provide a temporary feeling, but contribution builds a lasting legacy. They understand something many people miss: peace does not come from buying more. It comes from building more value.

Another key difference is how they invest in themselves. Unshackled thinkers invest in their personal growth before anything else. They read. They reflect. They ask better questions. They search for mentors instead of distractions. They understand that being busy does not equal being productive. Hustle without strategy is simply exhaustion. If you want new outcomes, you must create new inputs. New ideas. New habits. New environments.

The Most Valuable Real Estate You Own

The most valuable real estate you'll ever own isn't land. It's the space between your ears. Guard it carefully. Train it intentionally. Feed it wisely. A disciplined mind produces greater returns than any investment account ever could.

What ultimately changed everything for me was simple. I stopped waiting for someone to rescue me. I stopped blaming circumstances. I started taking responsibility for my thinking. Not just my actions, but my thoughts. That's where real freedom begins. Sometimes the way out isn't a new opportunity. Sometimes it's simply a new way of thinking.

Change the way you think about money, and you begin changing the life your money can build.

CONSIDER

What generational money habits did you inherit? Many of us inherit financial patterns without realizing it. Some were helpful. Others quietly reinforced limitation. Identifying them is the first step toward replacing them.

Which financial habits do you want to stop? Breaking cycles requires intention. The habits that created financial struggle in the past do not have to define the future.

What new habits do you want to start? When you replace silence with strategy, you begin creating a new financial legacy for the generations that follow.

ACTION

What money belief have you been carrying that has been quietly shrinking what you think is possible for you? Name it. Then name the belief you're choosing to replace it with. Complete the following sentence:

Because I learned that money was

______________________________,

I now believe

____

________________.

Then ask yourself:

- Is this belief always true?
- Who taught me this belief?
- Were they financially where I want to be?
- What has this belief cost me?

Now replace the belief with a stronger one.

Example:

Limiting belief:
"Having large amounts of money is selfish."

New belief:
"I steward wealth with purpose."

Write your new belief somewhere you will see it often. Your environment should reinforce the future you want to create.

DOABLE

This month, read one book, listen to one series of talks, or have one conversation with someone whose financial thinking you want to learn from.

Write down the one idea that shifts how you see money.

Chapter 3: Wealth vs. Rich: Know the Difference

Wealth vs. Rich: Know the Difference

The world loves rich. It rewards flash. It applauds the car, the clothes, and the lifestyle. But what it rarely celebrates, and what truly matters, is wealth. Rich looks good. Wealth feels good.

The Trap of Looking Successful

For a long time, I chased rich. I believed that if I looked successful, I would eventually feel successful. If I played the role long enough, maybe the reality would follow. So, I bought into the lie that image equals freedom. But behind the nice things were quiet anxieties. Credit card bills. No real savings. And the constant pressure to keep performing. Rich was loud. Rich was exhausting. Rich was a mask.

The Quiet Power of Wealth

Wealth is built differently. Wealth grows quietly. It's built in early mornings when no one is watching. It grows through sacrifices nobody applauds, and small decisions repeated consistently over time. It means saying no to the moment and saying yes to the mission.

Eventually I had to face a hard truth. I didn't need more money. I needed a different mindset. Because wealth isn't simply a number. It's a way of thinking. It's ownership instead of appearance. Control instead of chaos. And peace instead of pressure.

A Conversation That Changed Me

One day Will, my best friend and accountability partner, looked me straight in the eye. I call him Big Money. He said something that hit me harder than any financial lesson I had heard before. "You are not going to outrun the long game. Stop trying to shortcut your way to a destination that only consistency can deliver." That moment hurt. But it healed something inside me too. I realized I was not broken. I was impatient.

Big Money was not trying to shame me. He was trying to free me. He helped me see that lottery tickets, impulse spending, and performance purchases were not wealth strategies. They were escape routes. And every time I took one of those shortcuts, I drifted further from real financial freedom.

The Long Game

Wealth is built in decades, not days. That message changed how I approached everything. Saving. Investing. Spending. Planning. I stopped chasing shortcuts and started building systems. My only regret is not starting sooner.

What Wealth Really Looks Like

Wealth is not flashy. You probably won't see it trending on social media. But in real life, it's priceless. Wealth looks like a paid off home. It looks like a stress-free trip to the grocery store. It looks like the ability to walk away from a toxic job or situation because your finances give you options. It looks like sleeping peacefully at night because the numbers finally make sense and the plan finally works. And wealth is not just about you. It is about the generations that follow.

Wealth teaches your children a different language. A language of ownership. Patience. And responsibility. It gives you the power to give generously, build strategically, and plan wisely.

The Difference That Changes Everything

Being rich is a moment. Being wealthy is a strategy. Rich fades. Wealth remains. When you truly understand the difference, something powerful happens. You stop trading your future for applause. You stop chasing temporary highs. And you start building permanent freedom. Real wealth does not need attention. It quietly whispers something far more valuable. You are safe. You have options. You are free.

Looking rich might impress people today. Building wealth gives you freedom for the rest of your life.

CONSIDER

Are your financial decisions rooted in ownership or optics?
Many financial choices are driven by the desire to appear successful rather than to build lasting security.

What story are you telling with your money?
Is it a story about appearances, or a story about freedom and stability?

What would change if you prioritized peace over projection?
Financial peace rarely comes from more spending. It comes from wiser decisions.

ACTION

Declare your wealth identity daily.

Begin affirming the financial identity you are building. Speak it in the present tense so your mind begins accepting it before your circumstances fully reflect it.

Words shape beliefs. Beliefs shape behavior. Behavior shapes your financial future.

Examples:

- I refuse to look rich today at the expense of being wealthy tomorrow.
- I build wealth quietly so my family can live freely.
- I choose ownership over appearances.

Speaking affirmations reinforces the mindset required for long term wealth.

Interrupt rich thinking when it appears.

Pay attention to the thoughts that surface when you make financial decisions. If the thought is driven by impulse, image, or instant gratification, pause and redirect it.

Example:

"I deserve this purchase."

becomes

"I deserve long term freedom."

That small shift strengthens your discipline.

Write two wealth affirmations of your own.

Keep them short and clear. Place them somewhere you will see them daily. Repetition turns intention into identity. And identity drives behavior.

DOABLE

Create a three-word mantra that represents your new financial mindset.

Say it daily. Let it interrupt old patterns and reinforce the future you are building. Mine? *Discipline Creates Freedom.*

Chapter 4: Buried by Debt: Built by Discipline

At one point in my life, I was buried under $95,000 in credit card debt. Not because I bought luxury cars or designer clothes. Because I made financial decisions based on ignorance and a fear of missing out (FOMO). I was in graduate school when some of my friends started talking about the stock market like it was their personal ATM. They were trading confidently. Boldly. Celebrating wins. And I wanted in. The problem was simple. I barely understood what a stock was.

Running Without a Map

No one in my childhood circles talked about investing. If someone mentioned the stock market, it was usually followed by the same sentence: "We can't afford that." But the truth is the opposite. Most people can't afford not to invest. At the time, however, I was the most inexperienced person in the room. And I still decided to run with the pack. I had no money to invest, so I did something reckless. I took cash advances from multiple credit cards at outrageous interest rates and poured the money into a brokerage account. Just like that, I was trading stocks. I had no strategy. No knowledge. Just adrenaline.

Have you ever been standing with a group of people and suddenly someone starts running? Everyone else starts running too, even though no one knows why. That was me. I didn't know where I was going. But I was running hard.

The Illusion of Early Success

At first, it worked. For a brief moment I was making $800 a day. To a young Army officer, that felt like proof I had discovered something special. I started imagining a completely different future. Maybe I could resign from the Army. Maybe I could become a full-time trader. Looking back, I thank GOD I never made that decision. Because what came next changed everything.

The Crash

It was late 1999. Right before the dot-com bubble burst. By that time, I had deposited the full $95,000 into my brokerage account. I had loaded up on penny stocks because that is what my friends were buying. Then the market collapsed. And I lost every dollar. All of it. It was the most expensive financial lesson of my life.

Climbing Out of the Hole

I didn't file bankruptcy. I didn't run. I stayed and fought. I consolidated balances. Transferred debt. Borrowed from Peter to pay Paul. Month after month. Payment after payment. It took years. During that time, life did not slow down. I had married young. Our first son arrived soon after. Our second son came five years later. We were raising two boys, moving across the world with the Army, and living paycheck to paycheck. Pressure stacked on pressure.

Debt does not only drain your bank account. It drains your mind. Your sleep. Your peace. But through that painful season I learned something powerful. Discipline is stronger than debt.

A Lesson That Came Full Circle

Years later, I found myself facing a completely different financial decision. In 2024, after years of being debt free and maintaining an 850-credit score, I made a calculated investment using a home equity line of credit. This time it wasn't reckless. It was strategic. Instead of chasing penny stocks, I invested in strong companies like Nvidia, Google, and Amazon. I invested the money gradually over four weeks, buying in tranches while the market was down.

One year later, the investment had recovered the entire amount and then some. The difference between those two experiences was not luck. It was discipline and knowledge. I no longer chased. I built.

Progress, Not Perfection

Today I don't trade on margin. I don't allow emotions to control my financial decisions. I follow systems. Automated contributions. Dollar cost averaging. Long term investing. This book isn't a story about perfection. It's a story about progress. You can be buried and still build a new future. But if you're wise, you'll learn from my mistakes so you never have to dig out of the same hole.

Debt may bury you for a season. Discipline can build the life that sets you free.

CONSIDER

Have you ever spent money to feel included, successful, or avoid being left behind?

What were you really buying, and what did it actually cost you?

ACTION

When you picture your full debt load right now, what emotions come up?

Write them down. You can't change what you refuse to name.

DOABLE

Stop digging. Commit to not using your credit card for the next 30 days.

Track every dollar you spend during that time.

Awareness creates discipline.

Discipline creates freedom.

Chapter 5: Winning the War Between Now and Later

We live in a world that celebrates speed. Two-day shipping. Instant streaming. Same-day delivery. Fast. Easy. Now. Somewhere along the way, that obsession with immediacy crept into how we manage our money. Especially for those of us who grew up with less, the idea of "later" often feels like a luxury we cannot afford. I know that feeling well.

For years I lived with the mindset that if something good came along, I had to grab it immediately. I was always looking for a shortcut. A workaround. A faster way to win. My ex-wife once looked at me with frustration and asked, "Are you ever going to change?" That question hit hard. Not because she said it, but because deep down I did not like the man I had become. That moment became my mirror.

The Shortcut Mindset

They say the apple does not fall far from the tree. My oldest son is an incredible young man. Respectful. Loving. Smart. But one day he tried to shortcut his way into luxury. CarMax was running a promotion. Buy a car, keep it for up to 30 days, and return it if you're not satisfied, as long as you stay under the mileage limit. My son bought a Jaguar. At a double-digit interest rate. He wasn't worried about the interest because he planned to return the car before the 30 days were up. In his mind he had discovered a loophole. A luxury car for a month for nearly nothing.

But when he returned the vehicle, he forgot to bring the spare key. He drove home to get it. That extra trip pushed the car over the mileage limit. CarMax refused the return. Now he owned the Jaguar. And he was sick about it. I was sick for him.

A Hard Conversation

I didn't bail him out. And that broke my heart. But I saw something in that moment. I saw myself. The same hunger for more. The same impatience. The same desire to win quickly instead of wisely. So, I sat him down and told him the truth. "Son, I get it. I used to be you. But this mindset will break you. Change it now, and everything changes."

The truth is simple. There are no shortcuts. And when it comes to money, shortcuts usually turn into setbacks. You think you are outsmarting the system. But most of the time, you are only outsmarting yourself. Real wealth is built slowly. Quietly. One disciplined decision at a time.

The Lie of Instant Gratification

For a long time, I believed I needed what everyone else had right now. I would look at my boss and envy his lifestyle. The house. The car. The clothes. What I didn't see were the decades it took to build it. I wanted the finish line without running the race. And that mindset was destroying both my peace and my progress. Instant gratification is seductive. It promises comfort. It promises excitement. It promises status. But it doesn't care about your future. It steals tomorrow to indulge today. Long-term thinking does the opposite. It sacrifices comfort now to create freedom later. That is what real financial independence looks like.

The Marshmallow Lesson

This principle has been studied for decades. In the 1970s, Stanford University conducted a famous experiment known as the Marshmallow Test. Researchers placed a marshmallow in front of children and gave them a choice. Eat the marshmallow now. Or wait 15 minutes and receive two. Some children ate it immediately. Others struggled but waited.

Researchers followed those children for years. The ones who delayed gratification tended to have higher academic performance, better health, and greater financial stability. The ability to wait turned out to be a powerful predictor of long-term success.

The Garden Principle

When I finally committed to building wealth, I realized something important. Money behaves like a seed. You plant it. You protect it. You water it with discipline. Then you allow time to do its work. I once taught this concept to a group of teenagers. Instead of using slides, I brought real soil, seeds, and small pots. I told them, "This is how wealth grows. You plant it. You nurture it. And you leave it alone long enough to grow." You don't dig up the seed every week to check if it is working. You trust the process. That's how wealth grows. Quietly. Patiently. Consistently.

The Small Decisions That Changed Everything

My financial freedom did not come from one big decision. It came from hundreds of small ones. The house I paid off. The 401(k) contributions I kept making. The vacations I delayed until I could truly afford them. The brand-new cars I chose not to buy. The paid-off car I kept driving instead of replacing. Those small decisions added up to something powerful. Freedom.

Choosing the Long Game

Don't let the world convince you that you're behind because you don't have everything today. You aren't behind. You're building. Every time you delay gratification, you invest in your future self. Eventually something changes. Those impulses stop controlling you. And what you gain is far greater than any impulse purchase. You gain control.

The Power of Starting Now

That transformation didn't come from a single book or podcast. It came from thousands of disciplined decisions. Over time, discipline became a habit. Then the math started working in my favor. I've always loved numbers. But when I truly understood compound interest, everything clicked.

When I saw the numbers for myself, I believed it. Investing $400 per month at 8 percent for 20 years grows into serious money. That realization changed my life. My only regret is not starting sooner. The best time to invest was yesterday. The next best time is today. "If you do what is easy, your life will be hard. If you do what is hard, your life will be easy." —Les Brown

So, ask yourself a simple question. Do you want quick satisfaction or lasting security? One feeds your ego. The other builds your life. Choose patience. Choose discipline. Choose the long game.

The battle between "now" and "later" is the quiet war that determines your financial future. Win that war, and you win your freedom.

CONSIDER

Are your financial habits helping your future or feeding your cravings?
Behind many impulse purchases is a deeper desire to feel better, feel successful, or feel in control. What would it look like to care for your future self with that same urgency?

Think about a moment when you could have waited but did not.
What did that decision cost you financially or emotionally? Let the lesson guide you forward instead of defining you.

ACTION

Write down every place your money went last month. Then put each expense in one of two columns: Future Self or Present Comfort.

Look at the totals. What does this tell you that you didn't already know?

DOABLE

Create a 24-hour pause rule.

The next time you feel the urge to make an impulse purchase, wait 24 hours. Most "needs" disappear with time. Use that pause to ask one question: "Is this decision moving me closer to the life I want?" Sometimes the most powerful financial move you can make is simply waiting.

Chapter 6: Mindset Is the Multiplier

Mindset Is the Multiplier

Mindset is the foundation of everything in life. Money. Opportunities. Challenges. Successes. Failures. All of them are shaped by how you think. Your mindset acts like a lens through which you interpret the world. When your thoughts are negative, negativity grows around you. When your thoughts are hopeful and disciplined, opportunity becomes easier to recognize. The difference isn't luck. It's perspective. The phrase I often use is simple. Life happens for you, not to you. That single shift changes everything.

The Power of Belief

Scripture says: "As a man thinks in his heart, so is he." — Proverbs 23:7 If you continually declare failure over your life, you begin to believe it. That belief shapes your decisions. Your decisions shape your actions. And your actions create your results. But the opposite is also true. When you declare success, discipline, and growth over your life, your behavior begins to align with that belief. Your mind starts building the life you expect.

The Subconscious Mind

Much of our behavior is controlled by the subconscious mind. When you repeat something often enough, it becomes automatic. Think about driving. Have you ever arrived at your destination and realized you barely remember the drive? Your subconscious mind handled most of the work.

The same thing happens with your habits. If you constantly tell yourself:

"I'm broke."
"I'm bad with money."
"I'll never get ahead."

Your subconscious mind begins to accept those statements as truth. Eventually your behavior reflects them. That's why your inner dialogue matters. What you repeat consistently becomes what you believe. And what you believe eventually becomes what you do.

Guarding Your Mind

The thoughts you feed your mind matter. Especially before sleep. The final thoughts you carry into the night often settle deep into your subconscious. Are you replaying the negative events of the day? Or are you focusing on gratitude and possibility? What you think about consistently begins to shape your reality. Not magically, but behaviorally. Your thoughts influence your actions. Your actions shape your life.

A Lesson About Character

I learned an important lesson about mindset through a conversation with my brother Daryl. One day I was venting to him about our other brothers, Robert and Patrick. Daryl sat quietly and listened. He barely said a word. Finally, I asked him, "When I'm not talking with you, do you think I'm talking about you?" He answered immediately. "Absolutely!" That moment stopped me in my tracks. I realized something important. The habits we allow into our lives eventually define us. That was the day I decided to stop gossiping.

A Leadership Principle

Today, if someone approaches me at work with a complaint about another colleague, I ask a simple question. "Have you spoken directly to them about it?" If the answer is no, I encourage them to start there. And if they still want to discuss the situation afterward, I ask that both parties be present. Most of the time the problem disappears. People often complain about situations they are unwilling to address directly. I prefer honesty. If someone has an issue with me, I would rather hear it from them than from someone else.

The Golden Rule

I try to live by the Golden Rule. Treat others the way you want to be treated. Attitudes are contagious. The mindset you carry into a room influences everyone around you. A negative attitude spreads quickly. But so does a positive one. Choose carefully.

Choosing Your Philosophy

Jim Rohn once said that every person chooses their philosophy of life. Your philosophy determines how you respond when things become difficult. My philosophy is simple. I will give my very best effort in every situation. That does not guarantee success. But it guarantees self-respect. And there is something powerful about knowing you gave your best. That confidence strengthens your mindset.

Change the Roots

One of the most influential books I ever read was *Secrets of the Millionaire Mind* by T. Harv Eker. He explains a powerful idea. "Change the roots, change the fruits." If you want different results, you must change the beliefs producing those results. Imagine printing a document that contains a typo. If you erase the typo on the printed page but do not fix the file on your computer, the typo will appear again when you reprint it.

Your thoughts work the same way. If you want to change your behavior, you must change what is happening inside you first. Pressure reveals what is already within us. Just like squeezing an orange produces orange juice, pressure in life reveals the mindset *inside* you.

Protecting Your Mind

Today I'm very intentional about what I allow into my mind. I rarely watch television except for college football and the NFL. I don't listen to the radio. Instead, I fill my mind with:

Educational podcasts
Uplifting music
Positive teachings

I study thinkers like Jim Rohn and Neville Goddard who emphasizes protecting your mental environment. Your mind is like a projector. Whatever you focus on today eventually appears on the screen of your life tomorrow. Dreams. Fears. Goals. Problems. Choose carefully.

Consistency Unlocks Opportunity

I believe GOD rewards consistency. When your mindset aligns with disciplined action, doors begin to open. Opportunities appear. The right people show up. But those things happen after you demonstrate commitment. Consistency proves seriousness. That's why I train both my mind and body every day.

Speaking Life

Since 2008 I have repeated a personal confession that reminds me who I am and what I stand for. I speak life over my situation. I speak blessings over my sons. I speak purpose over my future. You'll find the full confession in the appendix. Because words matter. The words you speak will shape the life you live.

Your mindset multiplies everything in your life. Feed it discipline and faith, and it will multiply opportunity. Feed it doubt, and it will multiply limitations.

CONSIDER

Think about the last raise, bonus, or windfall of money you received. What did you do with it?

Did it build your net worth or improve your lifestyle? What does your answer tell you about where your focus has really been?

ACTION

Define Your Personal Philosophy

Every person lives by a philosophy whether they realize it or not.

Ask yourself:

- What kind of person do I choose to be when life is difficult?
- What values guide my financial decisions?
- What standards will I refuse to compromise?

Write a short statement that defines your philosophy.

Example:

"I choose discipline over distraction, ownership over excuses, and growth over comfort."

Your philosophy becomes your compass. When difficult decisions appear, it reminds you who you decided to become.

DOABLE

Start a 30-Day Financial Discipline Challenge

Choose one expense that quietly drains your money each month.

Examples: Subscriptions. Takeout meals. Impulse purchases. Convenience spending. Eliminate that expense for 30 days. Instead of spending the money, redirect it into savings or investments. Two things will happen. First, you will discover that the expense was not truly necessary. Second, discipline will create momentum. At the end of 30 days, calculate how much money you redirected toward your future. That is mindset in action.

Chapter 7: The Power of Purposeful Giving

I used to think generosity was something you arrived at. Something you did after you had "enough." After the bills were paid. After the savings account was full. After the investments were working. But I eventually learned something powerful. Generosity is not the destination. It's the vehicle. The sooner you begin giving with purpose, the further your life travels. Not just financially, but emotionally, spiritually, and generationally.

Giving Develops You

Purposeful giving doesn't deplete you. It develops you. It teaches you that you don't have to wait for wealth to make an impact. In fact, giving before you feel ready is often what breaks the grip of fear and scarcity. Giving trains your mind to live beyond survival. It shifts your focus from what you lack to what you can build. When that shift happens, everything changes.

From Survival to Significance

There was a season in my life when I believed I could not afford to give. Looking back, the truth is the opposite. I couldn't afford not to give. My heart needed something bigger than my own problems. I needed a reason to move beyond survival. That shift from survival to significance changed my life. When your giving becomes guided by purpose, your life begins to echo far beyond yourself.

Discovering Your Burden

Purposeful giving begins with a simple question. What burden are you called to help carry? That burden becomes your mission. Your mission shapes your priorities. Eventually your money begins to work for something that outlives you.

The Birth of Be the Best Foundation

When I founded Be the Best Foundation, it wasn't because I had extra money sitting around. It was because I couldn't ignore the need any longer. I saw too many Black boys falling through the cracks. Young men who lacked mentors. Young men who lacked hope. Communities where financial literacy was almost nonexistent. I wanted to give them more than advice. I wanted to give them access. So, the foundation was born. It started from brokenness. But it became the beginning of legacy.

When Giving Multiplies

We gave what we had. Mentorship. Financial literacy tools. Scholarships. Guidance. And we watched it multiply. Lives changed. Confidence grew. Cycles began to break. What started as a small act of obedience became something I pray will outlive me.

Generosity Is Modeled

Giving did not just bless the young men we served. It changed me. It reshaped how I think about money. It redefined success. And it influenced my sons. I remember teaching Corey to tithe when he was just a toddler. Later I watched him teach his younger brother Jared to do the same. That moment reminded me of something important. Generosity is not inherited. It's modeled. Children learn generosity by watching it.

Giving Is Bigger Than Money

Giving isn't only about dollars. It's also about: Time. Talent. Wisdom. Encouragement. Advocacy. Sometimes the most powerful gift you can give someone is belief. Belief in their future. Belief in their potential. Belief that their life can become something greater. Especially when they do not believe it yet themselves.

Living Open-Handed

I once heard a lesson that changed how I think about giving. Someone asked me to clench my fist. Then they asked a simple question. "What can you give with a closed hand?" Nothing. Then they asked another question. "What can you receive?" Again, nothing. That moment reframed everything. Closed hands cannot give. Closed hands cannot receive. So, I choose to live open-handed. Because only open hands can both release blessings and receive them.

Make Giving Part of Your Plan

Giving shouldn't be an afterthought. It should be part of your financial plan. Just like saving. Just like investing. Just like budgeting. Purposeful giving isn't charity alone. It's alignment. Alignment between your values and your resources. When your giving reflects what matters most to you, money takes on deeper meaning.

Teaching the Next Generation

Teach your children generosity early. Let them see you give. Let them participate in the process. Explain why it matters. A generous child often becomes a grounded adult. And grounded adults build more than wealth. They build legacy.

Success vs. Significance

The world has plenty of people chasing success. Titles. Income. Recognition. But what the world needs is more people chasing significance. More open hands. More open hearts. More intentional givers who aren't waiting for someday. Because they've already decided to start today.

Wealth measures what you keep. Significance measures what you give. The most powerful lives learn to build both.

CONSIDER

Are you waiting for financial security before you begin giving?

What if generosity today is part of what builds the security you seek tomorrow?

Who invested in you when you had little to offer in return?
How might your generosity honor the people who helped shape your life?

ACTION

Reflect on moments when generosity blessed your life.

Write down:

- Times you gave
- Times someone gave to you
- The impact those moments created

Let that list remind you that generosity expands your life in ways money alone never could.

DOABLE

Start a monthly recurring gift this week. It doesn't have to be large. Even $10 a month given consistently is more powerful than $100 given once. Set it up today. Write down who you're giving to and why. Let generosity become a rhythm, not a reaction.

Chapter 8: Budget Like a Millionaire

Building wealth doesn't begin with luck. It begins with leadership. Not leadership of others, but leadership of yourself. And that starts with how you manage the money you already have. Wealth isn't built by income alone. It's built by behavior. That's the real millionaire mindset.

Wealth doesn't fall into your lap. It's cultivated through clarity, consistency, and commitment. A budget isn't a punishment. It's a money map for power. It allows you to direct your dollars instead of wondering where they went. It's not a cage. It's a compass. For me, it became a lifeline.

Learning Money the Hard Way

The truth is, I didn't grow up with financial wisdom. I didn't have a mentor showing me how to build a legacy. I had to fight for every lesson. One overdraft, one late payment, and one financial bruise at a time. I learned money the hard way. Black eyes. Busted lips. Hard lessons. More than once, I almost gave up.

I've sat in my car after work with my paycheck already spoken for before it even hit my account. I've wondered how I was going to stretch fifty dollars to cover the rest of the week. I've looked success in the eye while still feeling like I was failing, simply because I didn't understand how to manage what I'd earned. But I refused to stay down. I refused to be defined by lack. That refusal became my strength.

The Mindset Shift

Eventually something changed. I stopped chasing quick wins and started playing the long game. I stopped living in survival mode and began building in purpose mode. I stopped saying "one day" and started saying "day one." That shift didn't happen overnight. It took years of falling forward. Years of trial and error. Years of unlearning old habits and rewiring my mindset. Eventually I realized something powerful. Budgeting isn't for the broke. It is for the bold. Budgeting is the tool that turns chaos into control and fear into freedom.

How to Build Your Money Map

Here are the basics. Create a budget/money map based on how often you get paid. Some people prefer bi-weekly budgets, while others prefer monthly budgeting. I personally prefer monthly because most major bills arrive monthly. Start by listing your income. Then list your expenses in priority order. Needs should always come before wants. The number at the bottom of your budget must be positive. If it is not, Houston, we have a problem! Below is an example of a simple monthly money map.

Sample Monthly Money Map

Income $7,830
Rental Property Income $2,600

Tithes .... -$1,043
Food .... -$500
Mortgage .... -$2,100
Homeowners Association Fees .... -$633
Electric Bill .... -$175
Gas Bill .... -$25
Insurance (Home / Auto / Life) .... -$440
Investments (Pay Yourself First) .... -$2,300
Gas (Auto) .... -$300
Cell Phone .... -$50
Mister Car Wash .... -$44
Fitness .... -$31
Spotify .... -$13
Disposable / Fun .... -$1,300

Balance (or Debt Eliminator) $1,476

Always list expenses in priority order. If you must remove something from your budget, start at the bottom because those are your lowest priorities. If the balance is negative, you must make adjustments. Begin by removing lower-priority expenses or increasing your income. Yes, increasing your income may mean taking on another job or pursuing a higher-paying opportunity. The fastest way to change a negative balance on your money map is simple: increase your income <u>and</u> decrease your expenses.

Budgeting gave me my life back. It brought clarity when everything felt foggy. It helped me spend on purpose instead of by impulse. It taught me that peace is worth more than possessions. A budget isn't about deprivation. It's about alignment. It ensures your money reflects your values. When your spending aligns with your goals, something powerful happens. You stop feeling anxious about money and start feeling confident about your future.

Even today, I review my budget every quarter. Life changes. Income changes. Priorities change. A good budget should adapt as your life evolves. A strong budget isn't rigid. It's responsive.

If you don't tell your money where to go, it will quietly disappear.

CONSIDER

Look at the last 30 days of your spending. How much went toward things that will matter in five years?

How much went toward things you barely remember buying? What does that split tell you about what your habits are really building?

ACTION

Create a simple budget this week.

Start by writing down your total monthly income. Next, list your fixed expenses. Then assign a purpose to every remaining dollar.

When every dollar has a mission, your money stops wandering and starts working.

DOABLE

This week, set up one automatic transfer. It can go to savings, a debt payment, or an investment account.

Pick the amount, set the date, and let it run. Write down what you automated and how much. Automation turns intention into identity.

Chapter 9: Destroy the Debt Before It Destroys You

Debt does more than slow you down. It suffocates your potential. It's not just a number on a statement. It becomes a narrative that quietly tells you what you cannot do, where you cannot go, and who you might never become. Over time, debt begins rewriting your future in someone else's handwriting. Debt is one of the greatest opponents to wealth. I know because I've lived it.

At one point, I owed nearly $100,000 in credit card debt. Not because I was living recklessly, but because I was trying to build a better life without a blueprint. I chased opportunities, hoping something would break through. Instead, I found myself stuck in survival mode. I was drowning in shame. I avoided looking at statements. I convinced myself I'd failed not only myself, but my family as well.

Debt is a thief. It steals your confidence. It steals your sleep. It steals your peace. And perhaps worst of all, it can convince you that this is simply how life will always be. But that's not true. You can change your story. You don't have to live like this. You can fight back strategically and win. Freedom begins with a decision. Not perfection. Not overnight success. A decision to face the numbers. To name them. To stop hiding from them. That is where your power begins.

Two Proven Debt Elimination Strategies

There are two widely used strategies for eliminating debt: the **Snowball Method** and the **Avalanche Method**. The Snowball Method asks you to list your debts from smallest balance to largest. You make the minimum payment on every debt, but you apply any extra money—what I call your **Debt Eliminator**—to the smallest balance with intensity. When that first debt disappears, you roll that entire payment, plus your

Debt Eliminator, into the next debt. Then the next. And the next. The goal is momentum. Each victory fuels the next one, and the psychological boost keeps you moving forward.

The Avalanche Method takes a more mathematical approach. Instead of organizing debts by balance, you list them by interest rate from highest to lowest. You still make the minimum payments on every debt, but you direct your Debt Eliminator toward the debt with the highest interest rate. Once that one is eliminated, you move to the next highest rate and continue the process until every balance is gone. This approach saves the most money over time.

Which Method Should You Choose?

So which strategy is better? The one you will actually follow. I've seen people win with both. The key is commitment. Choose a strategy, stay consistent, and refuse to quit until you are free. On paper debt elimination looks simple. But what's easy to understand is often difficult to execute. Discipline, patience, and sacrifice are required. The more consistent you become, the faster you will begin to feel the chains loosen. You weren't born to live in chains. You were created to build, to lead, and to thrive. But that's difficult to do while carrying the weight of financial obligations that never seem to disappear.

So cut the anchor. List every debt. Choose your strategy. Sacrifice for a season. Sell things you don't need. Pick up additional work if necessary. Delay instant gratification. Every disciplined action becomes a brick in the foundation of your freedom. Destroy the debt before it destroys you. Become unshackled.

Destroy the Debt Before It Destroys You

CONSIDER

What debt causes you the most stress?

What was the last thing you put on credit that you didn't truly need?

What were you trying to feel or avoid feeling when you bought it?

What payoff strategy fits you best and why?

ACTION

Stop digging.

The first step to escaping a debt hole is to stop digging deeper. That means stopping the habit of spending on credit. This may feel difficult at first. But living paycheck to paycheck is difficult too. Continuing to carry the stress of mounting debt is difficult.

There is no painless shortcut out of the hole. The path forward requires discipline and honesty. Different actions will create different outcomes.

Next, choose your strategy. Snowball or Avalanche? Plan your first three debt attacks. Identify the specific account you will target, the amount you will apply, and the timeline for progress. You do not have to eliminate every debt today. But you must begin.

DOABLE

Use your Debt Eliminator.

Look at your budget from Chapter 8 and identify the amount available to attack your debt each month. Direct that money toward your chosen strategy, either Snowball or Avalanche. The more aggressively you apply those funds, the faster your balances will disappear. You are declaring war on your debt. Every dollar redirected is a dollar reclaimed for your freedom.

Chapter 10: FICO Score: The Silent Wealth Gatekeeper

Fair Isaac Corporation (FICO), founded in 1956 by Bill Fair and Earl Isaac, is the analytics company behind the credit score system that shapes the financial opportunities of millions. Your FICO score functions like a silent résumé. It speaks for you when you're not in the room. This unassuming number carries enormous influence. It affects decisions about loans, housing, and sometimes even employment.

You don't need a perfect score, but you do need a smart one. A strong FICO score can lower your interest rates, increase your credit limits, and unlock financial doors that poor credit keeps firmly closed.

FICO scores range from **300 to 850**:

300–579: Poor
580–669: Fair
670–739: Good
740–799: Very Good
800–850: Excellent

The closer your score moves toward 850, the more favorable the financial terms you will typically receive. Your score is calculated using five key factors:

Payment History — 35% (Do you pay on time?)
Credit Utilization — 30% (How much of your available credit are you using?)
Length of Credit History — 15%
Credit Mix — 10% (Credit cards, student loans, auto loans, etc.)
New Credit Inquiries — 10%

It's not magic. It's math. And math doesn't lie. Once you understand the formula, you can begin moving the number in your favor.

My Journey to an 850 Credit Score

For years I ignored my credit score. I believed that unless I was buying a house or a car, it didn't matter. I was wrong. Better credit creates better options. And when it comes to building wealth, options matter. I remember checking my score during one of the lowest financial periods of my life. It was under 650. Seeing that number stung. But that moment also sparked a commitment. I made a promise to myself that I would do everything in my power to raise my score to 850.

Why? Because I wanted to live out my mother's mantra: **Be the Best.** And eventually, it happened. In 2023 I logged into one of my credit card accounts and saw the number staring back at me: **850**. I could hardly believe it. I wanted to shout, celebrate, and reflect on the long journey that had brought me there. I checked my score through other credit monitoring tools. Not every source showed the same number, but two of the three credit bureaus confirmed it. I had reached the top.

There are three major credit bureaus—Equifax, Experian, and TransUnion—and their scores sometimes differ slightly. But when two of them reported 850, I knew I had achieved my goal.

Then life tested me again. I withdrew $65,000 from my Home Equity Line of Credit (HELOC) and invested it in the stock market. My credit score immediately dropped below 775. But when I paid the balance off, the score rebounded to 850 within about 45 days.

Today, I protect my FICO score carefully. I avoid borrowing money unless it's absolutely necessary, and I often pay off credit card charges the same day I make them.

Protecting Your Credit Reputation

Your credit score can save or cost you tens of thousands of dollars over your lifetime. It's not just a number. It's leverage. A strong credit profile signals that you manage financial responsibilities wisely. But your score is also vulnerable. One of the biggest myths you will hear is this: "We'll just do a soft pull.

It won't affect your score." Be cautious. Sometimes what begins as a soft pull ends up being recorded as a hard inquiry, and hard inquiries can lower your credit score. Always ask for clarification, and if possible, get it in writing.

Personally, I now assume that every credit pull will affect my score. Whether it comes from a car dealership or a mortgage lender, I treat it as a potential hard inquiry. Here's another helpful strategy. If you're shopping for a mortgage, complete all of your loan inquiries within a 30-day window. Credit scoring models typically count multiple mortgage inquiries within that timeframe as a single inquiry. This protects your score while allowing you to compare lenders.

Another common mistake people make is closing unused credit cards. At first glance this seems like a responsible move, but it can actually hurt your score. Credit utilization accounts for 30% of your FICO score. When you close a credit card, your total available credit drops immediately, while your existing balances remain the same. This increases your utilization percentage and can lower your score.

A better option is to cut up the card if you don't trust yourself to use it responsibly but keep the account open. You can also remove stored credit card information from online shopping accounts to reduce the temptation to overspend. And one more important warning. Never open credit cards in your children's names and accumulate debt under their identities. That practice is not only unethical, but also illegal. It damages their financial future before they even begin adulthood.

If you're reading this book, I believe you want something better for yourself and your family. Don't cheat the system. Learn the system. Work within it. Build your reputation over time. Treat your FICO score like a VIP pass. Protect it wisely and you'll find many more financial doors opening along your journey.

A strong credit score opens doors that poor credit quietly locks.

CONSIDER

Do you know your credit score right now, today, without looking it up?

If not, what decisions have you been making without knowing the number that's quietly shaping every financial opportunity available to you?

When you understand the financial system, you stop reacting to your credit score and begin managing it intentionally.

What opportunities might you be missing because of an average or low credit score?

Lower interest rates, higher credit limits, and better financial terms often go to those with stronger credit reputations.

ACTION

Check your credit report today.

Visit **AnnualCreditReport.com** and review your report from all three bureaus. You're entitled to one free report from each bureau every year. You cannot improve what you refuse to examine.

DOABLE

Protect your payment history.

Set up automatic bill payments whenever possible. Payment history makes up **35% of your FICO score**, and automation helps ensure you never miss a due date. It's a small step that creates a powerful habit.

Chapter 11: Save Like Your Life Depends On It

Saving is not optional. It's survival. It's how you breathe through the financial fires that life will eventually throw your way. If you don't start building that safety net now, there may come a day when you desperately wish you had. I didn't always understand this. For years, I believed saving was something only wealthy people could do. I assumed you had to have money first before saving even became possible. I was wrong. Saving is how you keep money. It's how you regain control when life feels uncertain.

When You Have No Cushion

I have experienced both sides of this reality. When I was broke, every small problem felt like a full-blown crisis. A flat tire could derail my entire week. An unexpected bill created instant anxiety. I would lie awake at night trying to solve financial equations that I already knew didn't work.

But something changed when I started saving, even in small amounts. Before I ever saw the impact in my bank account, I felt the difference in my chest. The money itself mattered, but the peace of mind mattered even more. That peace was priceless.

Preparing for Life's Inevitable Storms

Let's be honest about something. Emergencies will happen. That's not negativity. That's reality. Cars break down. Jobs disappear. Medical expenses show up uninvited. Family situations require sudden travel. No one is exempt. The question isn't *if* life will present challenges. The question is *when*. When those moments arrive, you don't want to panic. You want to respond with stability and confidence. Start small. Save your first $500. Then build toward $1,000. Eventually work toward three months of living expenses, and then six months. This isn't easy. But your future deserves stability. Your peace of mind is worth the sacrifice.

The Day Preparation Became Freedom

I will never forget the day I was let go from a job that I knew was no longer working for me. I could feel it coming. The tension. The meetings. The final one-on-one conversation with HR sitting in the room. But this time, something was different. I didn't panic. I had my military pension. I had a savings account. I had a plan. Losing my job didn't feel like a disaster. It felt like freedom. That moment became the catalyst for the best version of my life. But it only felt like a blessing because I'd prepared for the fallout.

Pay Yourself First

Maybe a voice in your mind is saying, *I cannot afford to save right now*. Let me gently challenge that idea. You cannot afford **not** to save. Even if it's only five dollars per week. Even if you have to search carefully through your spending to find it. Because saving does more than build a bank balance. It builds belief. Belief in yourself. Belief in your future. Belief that your life is worth protecting. That's why the phrase **"pay yourself first"** is so powerful. It's not just about money. It's about mindset. It's a declaration that your future matters.

Many of us were not raised with that mindset. I certainly wasn't. My family lived paycheck to paycheck for years, often wishing there was more money left at the end of the month. Everything changes when you make one new decision. Your future matters more than your impulses.

Guard Against Lifestyle Creep

Here is something else to watch closely: lifestyle creep. Every time your income increases, there will be pressure to upgrade something. A nicer car. Better clothes. Bigger vacations. But the goal isn't to look richer. The goal is to become freer.

Automation helps you protect that goal. Set your savings transfers to occur automatically. Base them on a percentage of your income, not a fixed dollar amount. That way your savings grow as your income grows. Make the process routine. Make it automatic. Make it boring. Because boring habits build extraordinary wealth.

Open a separate savings account and give it a name that motivates you. Call it something meaningful: "Peace Fund." "Freedom Account." "Legacy Jar." Protect that account as if it were sacred, because in many ways it is. That account represents your choices. Your confidence. Your future options. Touch it only during true emergencies or when you are ready to invest in something extraordinary.

Saving is how you take care of the version of yourself that hasn't arrived yet. It's how you love your future self before you ever meet them.

Save like your life depends on it.

CONSIDER

If a $1,000 emergency hit tomorrow, would you be prepared? Where would the money come from?

If the answer is a credit card, a family member, or you don't know, that answer is the reason this chapter exists.

What is truly preventing you from paying yourself first?

Is it fear? Habit? Or the quiet belief that you are not worth prioritizing? Replace that belief with truth. Your future is worth protecting.

What would it feel like to face a financial emergency with substantial savings?

That peace is possible. It begins with the habits you start building today.

ACTION

Open a separate savings account today.

Give it a name that means something to you: "Peace Fund," "Safety Net," or "Legacy Account."

Naming the account creates emotional connection. Emotional connection strengthens commitment.

DOABLE

Automate weekly or monthly deposits into your "emergency" savings account .

Even small deposits build powerful habits when they happen consistently. Automation removes the need for motivation.

Check your progress in 60 days and increase the amount if you can. Celebrate your discipline and increase the amount gradually. Keep saving. Set a goal to save one month's worth of expenses, then two months, and eventually six months' worth of expenses in your emergency savings account.

Every step forward sends a message to yourself: I believe in my future.

BONUS INSERT

The Investor's Pyramid

The biggest mistake new investors make is trying to start at the top. They want hot stocks.
Quick gains. Crypto windfalls. The next big thing. But wealth isn't built from the top down.
It's built from the **bottom up**.

Every strong financial life rests on a foundation. When the base is solid, the upper levels become powerful. When the base is weak, the entire structure eventually collapses. Here's what the pyramid looks like.

THE
INVESTOR'S PYRAMID

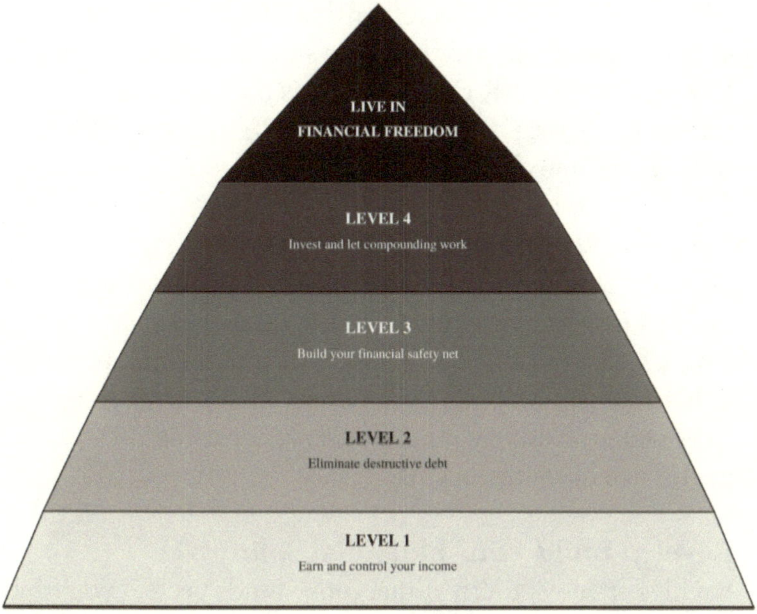

The Order of Wealth Building.

Wealth is not built by chasing the top of the pyramid. It is built by strengthening the foundation.

Building the Pyramid

Level 1: Earn and Control Your Income

Everything begins here. Income is the fuel for wealth building. Discipline determines whether that fuel is used wisely or wasted. Without discipline, more income simply leads to more spending. This is why the early chapters of this book focus heavily on mindset, budgeting, and delayed gratification. Wealth is not built by income alone. It's built by behavior.

Level 2: Eliminate Destructive Debt

Debt is one of the biggest obstacles to financial progress. High-interest debt works against you the same way compound interest works for investors. Every dollar going to interest payments is a dollar that cannot build your future. That's why destroying bad debt and protecting your credit score are essential steps before aggressive investing begins.

Level 3: Build Your Financial Safety Net

Savings create stability. Emergency funds protect you from life's unexpected challenges. They keep temporary setbacks from turning into long-term financial disasters. Savings also create breathing room. When you know you have reserves, you can make wiser decisions instead of desperate ones.

Level 4: Invest and Let Compounding Work

This is where wealth truly begins to accelerate. Once income, discipline, debt management, and savings are in place, investing allows your money to begin working for you. Your dollars start producing more dollars. And those dollars begin producing even more. This is the stage where compound interest and long-term investing strategies begin transforming ordinary incomes into extraordinary outcomes.

The Top: Live in Financial Freedom

Financial freedom isn't about luxury. It's about options. The freedom to walk away from toxic situations. The freedom to support your family. The freedom to give generously. The freedom to live life on your terms. And it all begins by building the pyramid from the ground up.

Wealth isn't built by chasing the top of the pyramid, it's built by strengthening the foundation.

Chapter 12: The Power of Compound Interest

"If you understand compound interest, you'll earn it. If you don't, you'll pay it." That phrase haunted me early in life, long before I truly grasped what it meant. Like many people raised in survival mode, I first learned about interest by experiencing its consequences. Overdraft fees. Credit card balances that grew faster than I could pay them down. Thank GOD I never took out Payday loans with enormous interest rates.

Compound interest wasn't a concept to me then. It was a curse. It took years before I learned how to flip the script. But once I did, everything changed.

Albert Einstein may or may not have called compound interest the "eighth wonder of the world," but I know this much: it's the quiet engine behind every wealth story that lasts. It rewards consistency more than brilliance. It honors time more than timing. It favors discipline over drama.

How Compounding Actually Works

Compound interest creates momentum. You don't just earn interest on the money you invest. You earn interest on the interest that money already earned. Then the process repeats. Money on money. Growth on growth. Over time, small decisions repeated with discipline can create staggering results.

Most of us didn't grow up seeing this in action. We didn't watch money multiply. We watched it disappear. Bills arrived quickly. Emergencies arrived even faster. So, when I say compound interest changed my life, I don't say that lightly. I didn't learn it in school. I learned it through struggle. Through trial. Through deciding that my children would never have to start where I started.

The Long Game

Consider this example. If you invest $5,000 per year at an 8% annual return, here is what happens over time:

After 10 years you will have contributed $50,000, but your account will already be worth over $72,000. After 20 years that balance grows to roughly $247,000. Stay consistent for 30 years and the value climbs to more than half a million dollars. Nothing flashy. Nothing complicated. Just time, consistency, and compounding. That's what happens when time and money become allies.

The Other Side of Compounding

Compounding works both ways. If you carry high-interest debt, the same force that builds wealth can quietly destroy it. A $10,000 credit card balance at 20% interest costs more than $2,000 per year in interest alone. That's not just lost money. That's lost freedom. Lost options. Lost legacy. You cannot build when you are buried.

A Legacy Moment

This is why I talk to my sons and any young person who will listen about compound interest. I started the conversations early. We talked about investing. I showed them charts. I planted the seeds. But like many parents, I sometimes wondered if the lessons were landing. Then one day my youngest son called me from his Army base. He'd just attended a financial class and said: "Dad, I finally get it. Will you please help me set up my Thrift Savings Plan?" That moment meant so much to me. Not because I needed credit. But because I saw legacy unfolding. A conversation I started had become a conviction of his own. And when he followed up asking about opening a brokerage account, I knew the lesson had truly taken root.

Try This Now

Open this calculator:

https://www.investor.gov/financial-tools-calculators/calculators/compound-interest-calculator

Enter the following:

$200 per month
30 years
8% return

The result may permanently change the way you see money. It reminded me of something important. The goal isn't to raise rich children. The goal is to raise children who understand how wealth is built. Children who do not just inherit money, but inherit the mindset required to multiply it.

Starting Today

If you're wondering when to start investing, here's the honest answer: Start now. Not when you feel ready. Not when the market looks perfect. Not when everything finally lines up. Just start. And if you're older and just beginning, that's okay too. Compound interest rewards whoever shows up and stays consistent. Even if you start later than you hoped, you can still finish strong. You don't have to be wealthy to build wealth. You simply have to be willing. Willing to act. Willing to learn. Willing to stay consistent.

Whether it's a savings account, a 401(k), a Roth IRA, a Thrift Savings Plan, or a brokerage account, set it up. Automate the contributions. Let it run quietly in the background while you keep showing up for your life. That's how ordinary people create extraordinary outcomes. Compound interest is quiet. But over time it becomes loud. It shouts freedom. It shouts options. It shouts legacy.

"The secret to wealth isn't brilliance—it's starting early, staying consistent, and letting time do the heavy lifting."

Compound interest turns patience into power.

CONSIDER

Right now, is compound interest working for you or against you?

Think about your debt balances growing and your savings sitting idle. Which force is stronger in your life today?

How many years have passed since you could've started investing but didn't?

You can't get those years back. But you still have today. What would it mean to start right now instead of waiting one more year?

ACTION

Use a free compound interest calculator online.

Run the numbers. Experiment with different savings amounts and timeframes. Let the math reveal what small decisions today can become in the future.

DOABLE

Teach compound interest to someone else.

• Show a child, friend, or family member a compound interest calculator.
• Enter an example together—such as $100 per month invested at 8% for 30 years.
• Ask them what surprised them about the result.

When you teach the concept, you strengthen your own commitment to living it.

Wealth multiplies fastest when knowledge does too.

Compound interest is the engine. In the next chapter, you'll learn exactly how to fuel it — consistently, automatically, and without relying on willpower.

Chapter 13: Invest Early, Often, and Automatically (Investing 101)

Knowing that compound interest works is one thing. Building a system that puts it to work for you — automatically, every month, regardless of how you feel — is another. That's what this chapter is about.. Saving protects your present. Investing builds your future. Your money must multiply. Investing is what allows that to happen. What is investing? Investing is simply ownership. It means placing your money into assets that have the potential to grow over time. Instead of letting your money sit idle, you put it to work so it can generate additional income for you.

People invest in many different types of assets, including:

• **Stocks.** Ownership in companies that grow and generate profits.
• **Index funds or Exchange Traded Funds (ETFs).** Collections of many stocks bundled together for diversification.
• **Real estate.** Property that can increase in value and generate rental income.
• **Retirement accounts such as 401(k)s or Roth IRAs.** Investment accounts designed to grow with tax advantages.
• **Businesses.** Starting or investing in ventures that create value.

You don't need to master every one of these today. What matters most right now is understanding a simple truth: Investing allows your money to grow while you focus on living your life. That's why the golden rule of investing is simple. Invest early. Invest often. Invest automatically. When those three habits work together, something powerful begins to happen.

Earn → Save → Invest → Compound → Freedom

This quiet formula sits behind most long-term wealth stories. Not luck. Not timing. Not hype. Just time and consistency.

The Power of Automatic Investing

One of the most common ways people begin investing is through an employer-sponsored retirement plan such as a 401(k). These plans make investing automatic. Every paycheck, a portion of your income is invested before you can even spend it. That simple system removes one of the biggest obstacles to building wealth: human behavior. When investing happens automatically, motivation and willpower are no longer required. The system works for you.

Many employers add an even greater advantage through *matching contributions*. Employer matching means your company contributes additional money to your retirement account when you invest your own. For example, a company may offer a 50% match on the first 6% of your salary that you contribute. Imagine you earn $60,000 per year. If you contribute 6% of your salary ($3,600) to your 401(k), your employer may add another $1,800. That's not investment growth. That's not market performance. That's ***free money***.

Very few opportunities in life offer an immediate 50% return before the market even moves. Yet millions of people leave this benefit untouched simply because they never take the time to understand their retirement plan. Don't coast through your own wealth-building opportunity. When I joined the team at North Hennepin Community College, they offered a strong retirement matching program. I went directly to Human Resources and asked for a complete list of the investment options inside the plan. Once I received the list, I researched each option carefully and made my selections. Looking back, that decision became one of the smartest investments I ever made.

Most employees never take that step. They sign paperwork during onboarding and move on with life, never realizing the opportunity quietly sitting in front of them. If your employer offers a match, capture **every dollar available**.

Building Your Own Investing System

Not everyone has access to a retirement plan with matching contributions. That's okay. You can still build your own automatic investing system using accounts such as:

- A Roth IRA
- A Traditional IRA
- A brokerage account

Most brokerage platforms now allow investors to automate monthly contributions the same way payroll deductions work in a 401(k). The key idea is simple. Create a system where investing happens consistently without requiring a new decision every month. When investing becomes automatic, wealth building stops feeling like a burden and begins functioning like a habit.

A Quick Word About Timing

Many people delay investing because they believe they must wait for the perfect moment. They wait for the market to drop. They wait for the economy to stabilize. They wait for the headlines to look better. But the truth is simple. The perfect time to invest rarely announces itself. What matters far more than perfect timing is building a consistent system that continues working year after year.

One of the most effective strategies investors use to accomplish this is called **Dollar Cost Averaging (DCA)**. It's a powerful approach that removes emotion, reduces the pressure of market timing, and helps investors stay consistent regardless of what the market is doing. Rather than trying to predict the market's next move, this strategy focuses on one principle: Show up consistently.

In the next section, we'll break down exactly how DCA works, why it has helped millions of investors succeed, and how you can apply it in your own life. Once you understand it, you may never view market ups and downs the same way again.

Bonus Insight

If you have the ability to fully fund your Roth IRA early in the year, research shows that investing the full yearly contribution sooner rather than later often produces stronger long-term results. Why? Because markets historically rise over time, and the earlier your money enters the market, the longer compound growth has to work. Time remains the most powerful force in investing.

A Final Reminder

Investing is not gambling. It's not hype. It's not emotion. It's not chasing whatever is trending this week. Investing is a disciplined strategy built on patience, knowledge, and consistency. More wealth is lost to fear and greed than to bad investments. Stay focused. Stick to the plan. Over time, that discipline turns into dividends. That's how real wealth is built. Not overnight, but steadily, year after year.

Most people don't fail at investing because they lack intelligence. They fail because emotions get involved. Fear during market drops. Greed during market rallies. Panic when negative headlines appear. These forces quietly sabotage even the best financial plans.

Before we explore one of the most powerful investing strategies ever created, it's important to understand the three invisible enemies that stop most people from building wealth.

The next section exposes them.

Consistent investing turns ordinary income into extraordinary opportunity.

CONSIDER

Does your employer match your retirement contributions? If yes, are you putting in enough to get the full match? If not, you're turning down free money every single paycheck.

That is your money. Go get it!

Have you ever bought a stock, a coin, or an investment because of a hot tip or a feeling rather than a plan? What happened? What's the difference between that and investing with a strategy?

Gambling is impulse and emotion. Investing is strategy and patience. Know the difference and live by it.

ACTION

Review your employer's retirement plan and confirm that you are contributing enough to receive the full employer match.

DOABLE

Choose one investing resource this week: a book, podcast, or article, and spend thirty minutes learning something new about investing.

Knowledge builds confidence. And confidence leads to action.

BONUS INSERT

The Three Enemies of Wealth

Most people don't fail financially because they lack intelligence. They fail because three invisible forces quietly work against them. These enemies destroy more wealth than bad investments ever do.

Enemy #1: Emotion
Fear during market drops. Greed during market rallies. Panic during recessions. Emotion causes investors to buy when prices are high and sell when prices are low, the exact opposite of what builds wealth. The market moves. Headlines scream. Emotions react. But wealth builders follow systems, not feelings. "The stock market is a device for transferring money from the impatient to the patient."
— Warren Buffett

Enemy #2: Market Timing
Many people believe wealth comes from buying at the perfect moment. So, they wait. They wait for the next crash. They wait for the next rally. They wait until things "feel safer." And while they wait, time passes. The truth is simple: No one consistently times the market. Even professional investors struggle to do it. Wealth is built through **time in the market**, not **timing the market**.

Enemy #3: Inconsistency
Starting. Stopping. Starting again. Investing a little one year, nothing the next. Jumping from strategy to strategy. Chasing hype. Wealth hates inconsistency. Compound growth requires patience and repetition. Small actions, repeated consistently over time, produce extraordinary results.

The Strategy That Defeats All Three

Dollar Cost Averaging (DCA). Investing automatically and consistently:

It removes emotion. It eliminates the pressure of timing the market. And it creates consistency automatically. It has helped millions of ordinary people build extraordinary wealth. The next chapter will show you exactly how it works.

"Wealth is rarely built in dramatic moments—it grows through quiet, disciplined habits repeated for decades."

Chapter 14: Dollar Cost Averaging (Investing 102)

One of the greatest enemies of investors isn't the market. It's often emotion. Fear when prices fall. Greed when prices rise. Panic when headlines scream recession. As you saw in the previous section, emotion, market timing, and inconsistency destroy more wealth than bad investments ever will. That's why one of the most powerful strategies ever created is also one of the simplest:

Dollar Cost Averaging.

Dollar Cost Averaging (DCA) means investing a fixed amount of money at regular intervals, no matter what the market is doing. Weekly. Monthly. Every paycheck. You invest whether the market is up, down, sideways, or making the evening news look scary. Over time something powerful happens.

When prices are high, your money buys fewer shares. When prices are low, your money buys more shares. Over time, the ups and downs average out, and you end up owning more shares at a lower overall cost. You don't have to guess the perfect moment. You simply show up consistently.

The Power of Not Guessing

Most people think successful investors are great predictors. They imagine wealthy investors staring at charts, perfectly timing when to buy and sell. But the truth is much simpler. Most successful investors win because they stay consistent long enough for compound growth to do its work. As the legendary investor Peter Lynch once said, "Far more money has been lost by investors preparing for corrections than in the corrections themselves."

Trying to time the market is like trying to predict the weather six months from now. Sometimes you'll get lucky. Most of the time you won't. DCA removes that pressure entirely. You don't have to predict. Just participate.

A Simple Example

Let's imagine you invest **$200 every month** into the same investment.

Month	Investment	Share Price	Shares Purchased
January	$200	$20	10
February	$200	$10	20
March	$200	$25	8
April	$200	$15	13.3

Total invested: **$800**

Total shares owned: **51.3**

Your average cost per share becomes roughly **$15.60**, even though the market price ranged from $10 to $25. That's the quiet magic of DCA. You buy more when prices are low and fewer when they're high without having to think about it.

When the Market Drops

Many people panic when the market falls. But disciplined investors see something different. They see **discounts.** When you are using DCA, market downturns become opportunities to accumulate more shares. More shares today can mean significantly larger gains when markets recover. What feels like bad news today often becomes one of the best buying opportunities you ever had. Legendary investor Warren Buffett once said, "Be fearful when others are greedy and greedy when others are fearful." DCA helps you live out that wisdom automatically.

The Hidden DCA System Most People Already Use

Here's something many people don't realize. If you invest through your employer's retirement plan, like a 401(k), you are already using DCA. Every paycheck, a portion of your income is invested. The market might be up that day. It might be down. It doesn't matter. Your money keeps going in. Month after month. Year after year. Without emotion. Without guessing. Without hesitation. And that consistency is exactly what builds wealth.

The Quiet Advantage

DCA may not look exciting. There are no dramatic headlines. No overnight fortunes. No viral TikTok videos. But over decades, this quiet strategy has helped millions of ordinary people build extraordinary wealth. And that's the real goal. Not excitement. **Freedom.** Freedom to walk away from stress. Freedom to support your family. Freedom to live life on your own terms.

One Line to Remember

If you forget everything else in this chapter, remember this:

Dollar Cost Averaging turns market volatility from an enemy into an employee.

CONSIDER

Are you waiting for the right time to start investing? What are you <u>actually</u> waiting for?

What would change about your financial life if investing happened automatically every month, whether you thought about it or not?

ACTION

You've been investing automatically for at least one month now. Pull up your account statement. Write down three things:

(1) the current balance

(2) how much you've contributed so far

(3) what the balance would be if you had waited another six months to start.

That gap between what you have now and what you would have had is the cost of delay. Keep it visible. Let it remind you why you never stop.

DOABLE

Start small. But start today (if you haven't already)

1. Choose an amount you can invest monthly (even $25–$100).
2. Set up automatic investing through your brokerage or retirement account.
3. Commit to continuing the plan for the next 12 months regardless of market news.

Momentum starts with the first step.

Chapter 15: Time In, Not Timing: Mastering the Long Game (Investing 103)

The Myth of Perfect Timing

I used to think wealth was about being smart enough to spot the right moment. But life taught me something far more humbling. Success isn't about perfect timing. It's about long-term commitment. It's about showing up even when it's slow, even when it's scary, even when the payoff feels out of reach. I learned that lesson the hard way.

The $95,000 Lesson

I once lost $95,000 chasing fast money in penny stocks.

Penny stocks are typically shares of very small companies that trade for just a few dollars. Sometimes just pennies per share. They often sound exciting because the price looks cheap and the upside appears enormous. But what most people don't realize is that many penny stocks trade in thin, lightly regulated markets where hype spreads faster than facts. Prices can spike quickly on rumors and collapse just as fast when reality catches up.

In other words, they are rarely investments. More often, they are speculation. I learned that lesson the expensive way. I didn't understand the risks. I let hype and urgency override logic I didn't yet have. That mistake crushed my ego, but it rebuilt my foundation. I stopped chasing luck and started trusting time. Thanks to Big Money, I finally started playing the long game. That shift changed everything.

Too many people are waiting for the "right time" to build wealth, start investing, or chase a dream. But waiting is often fear dressed up as strategy. Time in the game beats perfect timing every single day. The market will go up and down. Life will twist and turn. But if you stay steady, if you keep planting, watering, and showing up, your consistency will compound into something real.

A few months ago, I spoke with a group of teens about investing. When one young man said, “Investing feels like gambling,” I didn’t flinch. He was right. Investing does feel like gambling if you don’t have a plan. But when you educate yourself, stay consistent, and invest in solid companies for the long haul, it stops being a gamble and starts becoming a strategy.

Emotion Is the Real Risk

Emotion is what traps most investors. Fear tells them to sell too soon. Greed tells them to risk too much. I’ve been there. I’ve learned to lead with principles instead of panic. Wealth rewards the steady not the sensational. And this principle goes far beyond money.

Your health, your relationships, your calling. They all respond to the same rule: give it time. Nourish it daily. Show up when it’s inconvenient. That’s how real growth happens.

Lessons From the Next Generation

Let me be honest. Watching my best friend’s son dive headfirst into options trading brought back painful memories. He was eager, bright, but impatient. I tried to slow him down. He didn’t listen. He lost money. Not much, thankfully, but enough to make him pause and start learning. I told him, “That loss wasn’t failure. It was tuition. You just paid for a lesson.” And that’s what time gives us when we stay in the game: lessons that stick, growth that lasts, and a life we don’t have to recover from.

The Rule That Wins

If you’re trying to rush the win, ask yourself what you’re really chasing. Is it success? Or the feeling of being enough? Time doesn’t just build wealth. It reveals worth. You don’t need to prove anything overnight. You just need to keep going. The market doesn't reward the fastest investor. It rewards the investor who stays in the game the longest.

Discipline, not drama. Time in, not timing.

CONSIDER

Have you been waiting for the "perfect moment" to start?

Perfection is the enemy of progress. Start messy, start scared, but just start. The clock doesn't stop, but your dreams will if you wait too long.

Are your investing habits consistent or reactive?

Let strategy, not emotion, be your guide. Your peace of mind is worth more than chasing the next big thing.

What areas of your life need more time, patience, and nurturing?

Compound growth isn't just financial. It's relational, spiritual, and personal. Stay the course. Don't underestimate what time can build when paired with belief.

ACTION

Set up or review your automatic investments.

Even small, steady contributions become powerful over time. Automate your future so emotions don't sabotage it.

Take one small step toward a long-term goal this week.

Momentum doesn't come from waiting, it comes from movement.

Write yourself a daily anchor:"

Discipline, not drama. Time in, not timing." Put it somewhere visible. Let it ground your actions when the world tempts you to chase quick results.

DOABLE

This week, write 'I invest for decades, not headlines' somewhere you'll see it every day. Then take one concrete action toward your long-term vision: make a contribution, set up an automatic transfer, or open an account. Small. Consistent. Starting now.

Chapter 16: From Scarcity to Security: Why I Built Multiple Streams of Income

Why Multiple Income Streams Matter

For most of my life, I carried the weight of financial fear. The kind that keeps you up at night calculating bills in your head and wondering what happens if the paycheck stops. That fear drove me. It pushed me to think differently about money. Not just how to earn it, but how to make it last. I knew one paycheck was too close to zero. I didn't want to survive; I wanted to feel safe. That required building something stronger. Something resilient.

That's why I stopped chasing only active income and started creating multiple streams of income. Some that I worked hard for, and others that now work for me.

Passive income became my pathway to peace, not because it's effortless, but because the effort is intentional and front-loaded. You build it once, nurture it, and then it pays you back for years. That kind of income is quiet, consistent, and freeing.

This wasn't just about making more money. It was about protecting my family, reclaiming my time, and creating options when life throws a curveball. When you only have one source of income, a layoff or crisis can unravel everything. But when you have multiple income streams, you build a cushion. You buy time. You create choices.

The Principle

Financial security grows every time income becomes diversified.

What Multiple Streams Look Like in Real Life

Here's what it looks like in my life now:

- **Military Pension**: After 25 years in the Army, I receive a pension that reflects not just my service, but years of missed birthdays, deployments, and sacrifice. It's steady. It's earned. It's my foundation.

- **Rental Properties**: Real estate taught me patience and discipline. I didn't flip houses. I found good homes, took care of good tenants, and slowly built equity and passive income. I now have only one rental property and my tenant now covers the mortgage, and then some.

- **Basketball Officiating**: What started as a passion turned into a disciplined source of income. Officiating keeps me sharp, focused, and connected. It pays dividends of discipline, decision-making, fitness, and confidence. I can use that money for whatever I want because I don't need it to live.

- **Certificates of Deposit (CDs)**: I use tenant security deposits wisely by placing them in interest-bearing CDs. That provides assurance to the tenant that when they return the home to me, their security deposit is there and has gained interest that I return to the tenant as long as they've properly cared for my home. It's not flashy, but it works quietly in the background, earning while I sleep.

- **Stock Market & Options**: I studied. I learned. And eventually, I started earning real returns. In 2025, I earned over $100,000 from dividends and option-premiums alone. Dividends are payments from the company whose stock I own... like interest payments. Dividends usually vary between monthly, quarterly, and annually. Option premiums are payments that buyers pay me (the seller) immediately, so they can have **the option** to buy my stock for a specified price any time within a specified period. That didn't happen overnight. It came from staying committed when the market felt slow, uncertain, and risky. I found it more advantageous selling options than buying them.

The point isn't to replicate my blueprint. It's to show that it's possible. Multiple income streams aren't reserved for the wealthy. They're built by the intentional. And they don't begin with a financial windfall. They begin with mindset, sacrifice, and consistent action.

I didn't build this all at once. I started with one stream. Then another. Each one brought more stability, and eventually, freedom.

The Wealth-Building Flywheel

When you combine consistent investing with time and compounding, a powerful cycle begins.

Income
↓
Save
↓
Invest
↓
Dollar Cost Average
↓
Compound Growth
↓
Financial Freedom

Each step feeds the next. Momentum builds. Eventually, your money begins working harder than you do, and the flywheel keeps spinning long after the first push.

THE
WEALTH FLYWHEEL

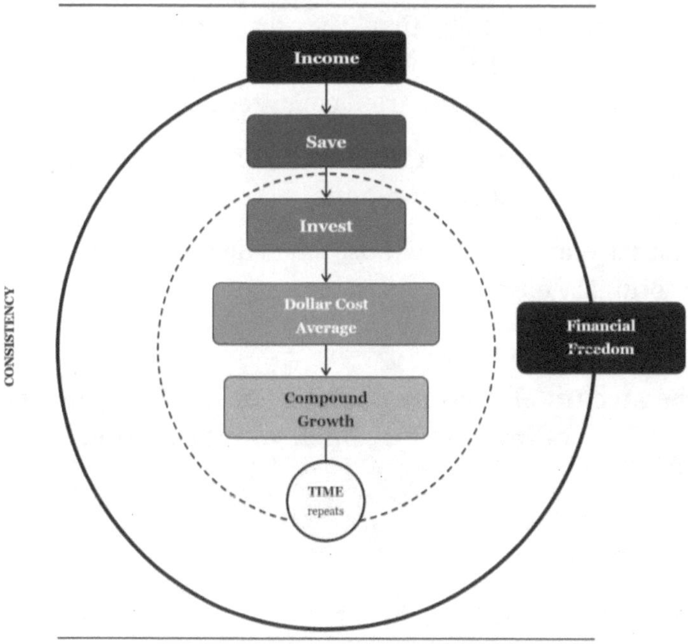

Consistency turns income into freedom.

Consistency Beats Perfection

Many people delay investing because they feel unprepared. They want to learn everything first. They want the perfect strategy. The perfect stock. The perfect moment. But wealth rarely comes from perfection. It comes from consistency.

You don't need to predict the next hot investment. You need to build a habit. Month after month.

Year after year. Over time those small decisions grow into extraordinary outcomes.

One stream of income pays the bills. Multiple streams of income buy back your freedom.

CONSIDER

If your job disappeared tomorrow, how long could you survive on what you have? What does your answer tell you?
Your answer isn't just about money. It's about peace of mind. One income stream makes you fragile. Diversification gives you options. And options bring freedom.

What skills or passions are you sitting on that could become a second income stream?
You don't need to start from scratch. You already have value. The work is in packaging it and committing to a plan.

Are you betting everything on one source of income?
That's not safety, it's exposure. Spread the risk. Protect your peace.

ACTION

Write down every way money comes into your life right now. Then write three more ways it could.
They don't have to be big. They must be real and doable within the next year.

Pick one income idea that genuinely excites you. Spend 30 minutes this week learning how someone else already does it.
Curiosity is the first step.

DOABLE

Commit to building one new stream of income, no matter how small.
Progress is not about speed. It is about movement. And movement builds confidence.

Chapter 17: Armor Up: Protect Your House

Why Wealth Must Be Protected

I've spent my life learning how to build discipline, wealth, and opportunity. But it wasn't until I saw people lose everything that I realized building isn't enough. You must protect what you've built. You can do everything right, you can save, invest, grow, and still watch it unravel in an instant if you're not protected. An illness, a lawsuit, an untimely death. That's not just a risk, it's a reality. And it's often avoidable. That's why I think of protection not as paperwork, but as armor. It's a shield around everything you love. Insurance. Wills. Legal documents. They don't just guard your assets they guard your peace of mind.

When I was younger, I carried term life insurance because I had people depending on me. A wife. Two sons. A mortgage. Responsibilities I couldn't afford to leave unprotected. That policy wasn't for me. It was for them. It bought time, tuition, shelter, and space to breathe.

Now I'm in a different season. I'm retired. My sons are grown. I'm debt-free. No one depends on my income to live. And that's the goal: to reach a point of financial maturity where you're self-insured, when your wealth becomes the safety net.

Let's be honest: most of us would never drive without car insurance. But too many walk through life uninsured against far greater risks including death, disability, disease. That's backwards. We can't predict the worst, but we can prepare for it.

As a military officer, I was covered. Healthcare, disability, all of it. But civilian life? It's a different story. I had to become my own protector. No one was coming to cover me. That realization lit a fire of responsibility in me! And about 'whole life' insurance? For most people, it's not worth it. I never understood paying interest to borrow your own money. That's why I advocate for term life, simple, cost-effective, and powerful when used well. Still, you should decide for yourself. Educate yourself. Don't wait. Because the longer you wait, the fewer options you'll have. And don't stop at insurance.

The Protection Map

Think of financial protection like layers of armor. Each tool protects against a different type of risk.

Income Protection

- **Health Insurance.** Protects you from medical costs that could wipe out years of savings.
- **Disability Insurance.** Replaces income if you're unable to work due to illness or injury.

Family Protection

- **Term Life Insurance.** Protects your family financially if you pass away unexpectedly within the covered term. It replaces income, pays off debts, and buys your loved ones time to adjust.

Asset Protection

- **Homeowners or Renters Insurance.** Protects your property and liability.
- **Umbrella Insurance.** Provides extra liability protection if you are sued beyond your normal policy limits.

Legacy Protection

- **Will.** Tells the courts who receives your assets and who will care for minor children.
- **Power of Attorney** (POA). Allows someone you trust to handle financial matters if you cannot.
- **Healthcare Directive or Living Will.** Tells doctors and family your wishes for medical decisions if you cannot speak for yourself.

These tools are not about fear. They are about clarity. They protect your family from confusion, courts, and chaos during the most difficult moments of life.

Protection Is an Act of Love

Real wealth isn't just built. It's protected. Wills, POAs, and healthcare directives aren't just legal forms. They're acts of love. They tell your family what to do when emotions are high and clarity is low. They remove confusion during moments when people should be grieving, not guessing.

I've completed mine. Because I've seen what happens when people don't.

Your wealth deserves protection. Your family deserves clarity. And your legacy deserves a plan. You didn't come this far to leave everything to chance.

Armor up!

Wealth that isn't protected is wealth waiting to disappear.

Building wealth is powerful but protecting it is what turns success into legacy.

CONSIDER

If something happened to you tomorrow, would the people who depend on you be okay financially? Do you know for certain?
Insurance is love in legal form. It shows up when you no longer can. If your car is better protected than your children or income, it's time to reset your priorities.

Have you delayed making a will or getting coverage because it feels uncomfortable?
Facing death is hard. But leaving your family unprotected is harder. Courage now creates comfort later.

You probably have car insurance. Do you have the same level of protection for your income, your family, and the wealth you're building?
Building wealth is only half the work. Guarding it is the other half. Don't ignore the shield while you sharpen the sword.

ACTION

Write down every protection you have: health insurance, life insurance, disability coverage, a will.

Don't guess. Look it up.

Pull out your insurance policies and read them.

When did you last update them? Does your coverage still match your life? Fix anything that has fallen behind.

DOABLE

Draft or update your will. Put power of attorney and healthcare directives in place.

Get a term life insurance quote today if someone depends on your income.
It's affordable and powerful. Every day you wait, it becomes more expensive and your risk grows. Protection is not pessimism. It's leadership.

Chapter 18: Understanding Taxes: Keep More of What You Make

Why Tax Literacy Matters

You cannot build lasting wealth if you do not understand taxes. Period. I learned that the hard way. Like many of us, I grew up with a fear of taxes. I thought of the IRS as something to avoid, not understand. I didn't grow up hearing about deductions, capital gains, or tax-advantaged accounts. I heard about debt. I saw struggle. When I finally started earning real money, I realized I was playing defense and watching large chunks disappear before I had a chance to use them strategically.

Here is the truth no one told me early on. The tax code is not just designed to take from you. It's built to incentivize you if you understand the rules. The tax system rewards behavior that builds wealth and strengthens communities: saving for retirement, investing in real estate, launching a business, and giving back. If you don't know what's available, you will keep overpaying instead of building faster and smarter. That is why tax literacy isn't optional. It's essential. When you understand it, you don't just save money. You reclaim power.

Top 5 Tax Truths I Wish I Learned Earlier

• Your salary is not your income.

Action: Use a paycheck calculator and ask HR to walk you through a sample pay stub before signing anything.

• 401(k) contributions reduce taxable income.

Action: At minimum, contribute enough to receive the full employer match.

• Roth IRAs grow tax-free.

Action: Open one early. Your future self will thank you.

• Holding investments longer than one-year lowers taxes.

Action: Long-term capital gains are taxed lower than ordinary income.

• Past filing mistakes can often be corrected.

Action: Ask a professional to review previous tax returns.

From Tax Fear to Tax Strategy

I used to think taxes were simply the price of earning money. Now I understand something different. The tax code is a roadmap. If you learn how to read it, you can accelerate your wealth-building journey and avoid unnecessary losses. I'm not saying taxes should be avoided. I'm saying they should be understood. I've sat across from too many hardworking people including veterans, entrepreneurs, and teachers, who overpay simply because no one showed them another way. We can do better. For ourselves, for our families, and for the next generation. Tax literacy turns the tax code from a cost into a tool.

CONSIDER

Do you think about taxes all year or only when April comes around? What has that approach cost you?

What habits could help you take control of your financial future?

You don't need to overhaul your life. Start with one change and repeat it consistently.

ACTION

Pull out your latest pay stub. Go line by line. For every deduction, write down what it is and how much it takes.

Most people have never done this. Do it now.

DOABLE

This week, schedule a meeting with a tax expert, not to file your return, but to ask how you can keep more of what you earn.

Do it before tax season starts.

Chapter 19: Legacy Building: Moving Beyond Yourself

Where Legacy Begins

At some point on your wealth journey, the question shifts. It's no longer, "How much can I make?" but "What difference will I leave behind?" That's the true measure of legacy. Legacy isn't just about dollars. It's about the depth of your influence. It's about the lives you touch, the cycles you break, and the future you shape for those who come after you.

THE
4 PHASES OF FINANCIAL FREEDOM

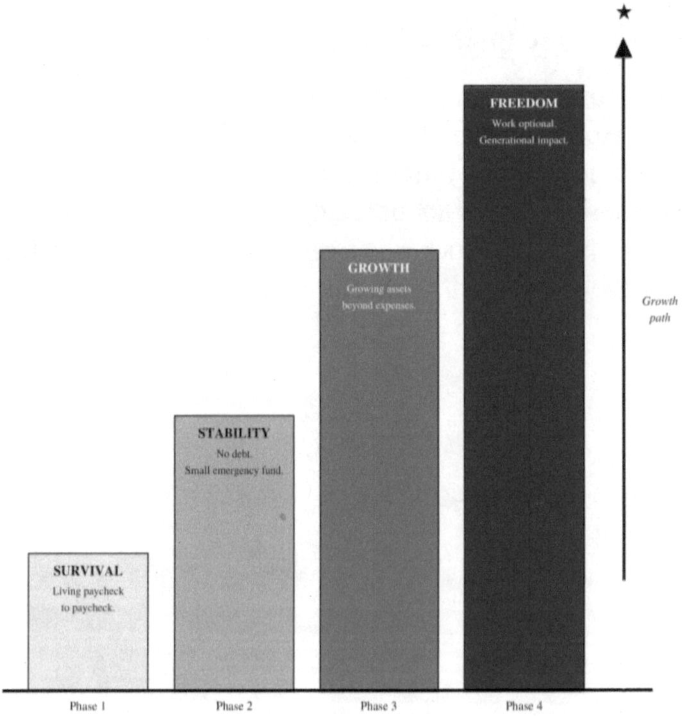

Rise above survival. Build for freedom.

Every financial life begins in Survival. Freedom is built one disciplined phase at a time.

The 4 Phases of Financial Freedom

Financial freedom rarely happens overnight. It unfolds through predictable stages of growth, discipline, and maturity. Most people move through these phases gradually as their knowledge, habits, and income improve. Understanding where you are today helps you see the path ahead.

Phase 1: Survival

This is where most people begin. Income barely covers expenses. Debt may be present, savings are limited, and financial stress is common. Decisions are often reactive because there is little margin for mistakes. The goal in this phase is simple: **stability**. You build discipline, learn to control spending, eliminate destructive debt, and begin creating financial breathing room.

Phase 2: Stability

In the stability phase, the chaos begins to settle. Bills are manageable. Debt is under control or disappearing. Savings begin to grow and an emergency fund starts protecting you from life's unexpected events. You are no longer drowning financially. You are learning to stand. This phase is where budgeting, saving, and disciplined habits begin transforming your financial life.

Phase 3: Growth

Once stability is established, wealth-building accelerates. Investing becomes a consistent habit. Your money begins working for you through compound growth, business income, real estate, or other assets. Your financial decisions shift from survival to strategy. Instead of asking "Can I afford this?" you begin asking "Will this grow my future?" Growth is where wealth begins multiplying.

Phase 4: Freedom

Financial freedom is not defined by luxury. It's defined by **options**. You have the ability to choose how you spend your time. Your investments and income streams support your lifestyle. Work becomes optional rather than mandatory.

Freedom allows you to focus on the things that matter most: Family. Purpose. Giving. Legacy. This is where money stops being the goal and becomes a tool for impact.

My Mother's Legacy

For me, legacy began with a woman who had a vision for a better world, my mother. She raised four boys in the ghettos of Mississippi, where poverty wasn't just a condition. It was a constant. No child support. Food stamps. Bill collectors on the line and figuring out which bill to 'let-it-ride' til next month. But despite all that, her spirit remained undefeated. Her message to us never wavered: "**Be the best.**" In school. In sports. In life. No excuses. Just excellence.

That mantra didn't just carry me. It carved me. It became my internal compass, pushing me through the honors curriculum, through combat zones, through boardrooms. To the rank of Colonel. CFO. VP. But the real title I carry with pride? Legacy bearer.

Legacy in Action

Out of that conviction, I created the Be the Best Foundation, named in her honor. It's not just a nonprofit. It's a movement, a living extension of her fire. Our mission is to equip Black youth and veterans with the tools to rise financially, emotionally, and purposefully. We don't hand out shortcuts. We hand out blueprints. Systems. Strategy. Support.

We teach adults and youth how to manage money because nobody taught us. We teach them how to avoid violence because too many of us didn't. We connect youth with mentors who carry both scars and wisdom. People who've survived the battlefield, the block, or the boardroom. If we don't reach youth early, the world will mislead them completely.

Legacy isn't what you leave to people. It's what you leave in them.

I don't build wealth to die rich. I build it to live richly and give freely. I've worked too hard, hurt too long, and healed too deeply to let my money sit passively. My wealth funds my purpose. It powers experiences with my sons. It fuels causes that move the needle. My boys have my time, my teachings, and my trust. I'm not stacking millions to pass down by default. I'm pouring it into people, into movements, into moments that matter.

I want to die with empty pockets but a full legacy. And if I do it right, the next version of me, some kid in a cramped apartment wondering if his life matters, won't need an inheritance. He'll already have the mindset. The method. The mission.

If I was only chasing dollars, I would've retired and vanished. But legacy won't let me rest. Legacy calls me higher. So, I keep moving. I mentor. I teach. I build. I show up. Because I'm not just making money, I'm making millionaires. And more importantly, I'm making missionaries of mindset. And I hope you do too.

Money builds comfort. Legacy builds meaning.

CONSIDER

What does legacy mean to you, not just financially, but in your heart and your faith? Are you building something that outlives you, not just in name, but in purpose?

Legacy isn't about ego. It's about eternity. It's how your values echo through the generations. Are you building something that outlives you—not just in name, but in purpose?

Who shaped your values? How are you honoring them today?

Legacy means looking back with gratitude and forward with intention. Who gave you the light you carry? How are you reflecting that light for others?

Are you chasing short-term wins or building something that will still matter 20 years from now? What is the difference between the two in your own life?
Short-term wins are easy. Generational change is sacred. The question isn't just what you're earning. It's what you're educating, elevating, and empowering.

ACTION

***Your legacy starts with your decision to align with your dreams.* Write a one sentence legacy statement.** "I want to be remembered for..." Let this become your compass, your filter, and your foundation for how you lead your life moving forward. Make it real. Make it vivid.

DOABLE

Share one financial lesson with someone younger this week.

BONUS REFLECTION

"Hard times create strong men.
Strong men create easy times.
Easy times create weak men.
Weak men create hard times."
— G. Michael Hopf

I think about this cycle more than I'd like to admit. I was forged during the hard times, raised by a woman whose strength was the only inheritance I received. I became a strong man, and by GOD's grace, I created easier times for my sons.

But here's the tension I wrestle with: I don't want my sons to become soft in the safety I built. I want them to inherit my resilience, not just my resources. That's the real challenge of legacy. Not just passing on money but passing on muscle. Not just leaving assets but leaving armor. That's the kind of legacy I want to leave. One that lives on in the fight, not just the fortune.

Chapter 20: Uncomfortable Obedience: You Weren't Created to Play Small

Dreams Require Movement

Shrinking your dreams can feel safer than risking disappointment. It's tempting to adjust your vision to match your current circumstances. But if you're called to build wealth, leave a legacy, and make a lasting impact, you can't afford to stay in that comfort zone. Big dreams demand bold moves.

And here's the truth: big dreams rarely feel comfortable. They stretch you. They expose your insecurities. They require you to become someone you haven't been yet. But dreaming alone won't change your life. Obedience will. Action will. Movement will.

There's a myth that successful people always had a plan. That they moved with certainty. But most of us? We were figuring it out as we went. We moved anyway. We trusted the vision, even when the path was unclear. Faith doesn't always come with a map. Sometimes it just whispers, *"Go."*

I've taken risks that scared me. I've made decisions that didn't guarantee success. I've failed. But I've also learned that fear doesn't get to drive. It might ride along, but it doesn't get to steer.

Dreaming big means setting goals that challenge your limits. It means becoming more disciplined, more resilient, more focused. Moving boldly means doing the thing you've been avoiding. Taking the course. Making the call. Launching the business. Applying for the grant. Saving the first $500. Making the first investment. It's not about being fearless. It's about being faithful in motion.

When Faith Requires Action

Recently, I had to live this out in real time. I was praying for next-level success, speaking affirmations, asking GOD for breakthrough. And then I heard it—*next-level results require next-level obedience*. I couldn't keep doing what I'd always done and expect something different.

That moment came when Be the Best Foundation was selected for funding consideration through a Minnesota state bill supporting Black veterans mentoring underserved youth. It was aligned with our mission, but accessing it meant stepping into unfamiliar territory. I had to testify at the State Capitol. Lobby legislators. Sit in rooms I didn't feel qualified to be in. I'm not a politician. But I knew staying comfortable wouldn't get us to the next level.

So, I showed up. Nervous. Uncertain. But obedient. And then came the news: the bill might only allocate $1,000—down from a proposed $5,000,000. It stung. But I stayed grounded. I stayed grateful.

Then, on a flight to Atlanta, I got a text from the bill's sponsor: the committee wanted to revisit the allocations. They asked for our high, medium, and low thresholds. That was divine confirmation. Even if the door only opened a crack, bold obedience had pushed it open.

Whether we receive $1,000 or $1,000,000, I'll keep showing up. Because obedience isn't about the size of the reward. It's about the strength of your *yes*. I'm still honoring my mother's charge: **Be the Best**. That means showing up with excellence, even when the outcome isn't guaranteed.

The Courage to Step Forward

Next-level results require next-level discomfort. You cannot stay where you are and arrive where you are called to be. You don't need perfect timing to pursue purpose. You just need the courage to take the first step. As Dr. King said, *"Faith is taking the first step even when you don't see the whole staircase."* So, take the step. Uncomfortable obedience might be the only thing standing between you and your breakthrough.

Comfort protects the life you have. Obedience builds the life you were meant to live.

CONSIDER

Have you been shrinking your dreams to fit your comfort zone?

Small dreams may feel safer, but they rob you of the opportunity to discover your full potential. Staying in that space may prevent you from ever experiencing the breakthroughs waiting on the other side of bold action.

What bold move have you delayed because it felt too risky or unfamiliar?

Avoiding the uncomfortable often delays growth. But the longer you wait, the more opportunity costs you rack up in income, confidence, and impact.

Where might GOD be calling you to step out, even if you don't see the full staircase yet?

When you move in faith, even with limited clarity, you invite divine alignment into your journey. Taking that step builds spiritual strength and invites momentum that fear could never produce.

ACTION

Write down a big dream that makes you nervous.

Then list one small move you can make toward it. Documenting your vision gives it life and breaking it into smaller steps makes it attainable. This approach reduces overwhelm and helps you stay consistent long-term.

DOABLE

Practice uncomfortable obedience this week.

Do the bold thing, even if the outcome isn't guaranteed. On the other side of discomfort is growth. Saying yes without full clarity opens you to blessings, favor, and strength that only show up after obedience.

Chapter 21: The Psychology of Money

Money Is Emotional

Money isn't just numbers. It's identity, memory, and emotion. It's a mirror of how we see ourselves, how we were raised, and what we believe we deserve. And if we never examine the psychology behind our money habits, we'll keep repeating the same patterns, no matter how much we earn or how many budgeting tools we download.

Throughout this book you've traced your financial origin story, examined generational beliefs, explored how those beliefs shape behavior, and discovered how deeply emotions are tied to every money decision you make. In this chapter we return to where it all began, because the psychology of money is not just about numbers, it is about the very human experiences that shape how all of us think, feel, and act around money.

Most of us are walking around with financial wounds we've never named. We spend to feel seen. We hoard because we're scared. We give too much because we're trying to buy love. We avoid looking at our bank account because we carry shame. Not just about what we spent, but who we think we are. That's why financial literacy isn't enough. You can know what to do and still not do it, because mindset always overrides mechanics. Behavior follows belief.

If you think you're bad with money, you'll act like it. If you secretly believe wealth is for "them" and not for you, you'll quietly sabotage every step forward. But if you believe you are capable, worthy, and resilient? You'll start behaving your way into a new financial identity. For me, one of the most transformative shifts came when I stopped asking, "Can I afford it?" and started asking, "Is this aligned with who I'm becoming?"

That question changed my life. It reframed spending from scarcity to strategy.

A Costly Lesson I'll Never Forget

Years ago, I got roped into a multi-level marketing pitch. I didn't even like selling. But I was tired, vulnerable, and wanted to feel like I was doing something "big." They convinced me to buy 13 water purifiers up front. "Flush them before you sell them," my upline said, "It'll save time with customers." So, I flushed them. Then found out the company wouldn't accept returns once they were flushed. I kept one. Gave one to my mom. A kind neighbor bought one. The rest sat in my garage, collecting dust and resentment. Hundreds of dollars gone. Money I didn't really have to waste. But the bigger loss wasn't financial. It was emotional. I realized I didn't buy those filters out of strategy. I bought them to be accepted. I wanted someone to tell me I belonged. That I was enough.

That moment taught me something I carry to this day: If you don't heal your relationship with money, you'll keep using it to solve emotional problems, and it will never be enough. That realization forced me to confront something uncomfortable. Money problems are rarely math problems. They're identity problems. They're belief problems. They're story problems. And the good news is this. Stories can be rewritten.

Rewrite the Story

We all inherited a money story whether we realize it or not. Who taught you about money? What did you observe growing up? What messages did you internalize about success, struggle, and worth? The truth is you didn't just inherit your last name. You inherited beliefs. But you are not defined by them. You can revise your story. You can choose a new narrative. And when you change the way you think about money, you change the way you experience life: your peace, your progress, and your purpose.

The moment you change your money story is the moment your financial future begins to change.

CONSIDER

What beliefs about money did you inherit growing up?
Many of our financial habits come from lessons we never consciously chose. Identifying those beliefs helps you decide which ones still serve your future and which ones need to be replaced.

What emotional experiences from your past are still shaping how you think about money today?
Money decisions are rarely just logical. They are often rooted in moments you experienced long before you understood them. Stress, lack, comparison, and even silence around money leave lasting imprints. When those patterns go unexamined, they quietly drive your behavior. But when you recognize them, you gain the ability to respond with intention instead of habit and begin building a financial life that reflects who you are becoming, not just what you have been through.

What new money story do you want to begin writing today?

Your past may explain your financial habits, but it doesn't have to define them. The power to rewrite your relationship with money begins the moment you choose a different narrative.

ACTION

Go back and reread chapters one through four. Read your origin story. Take time to reflect:

- Where it started. What you saw and learned about money growing up.
- What changed. The experiences, mistakes, or breakthroughs that shaped your thinking.
- Where you're going. The financial identity you're building now.

Clarity creates direction. And direction creates momentum.

DOABLE

Celebrate one financial win this week.

No matter how small. Saving $50, paying down debt, or saying no to an unnecessary purchase. Acknowledge the progress.

Chapter 22: The Comparison Trap: When Lifestyle Lies to You

Comparison doesn't just steal joy. It can steal your future.

The Illusion of Lifestyle

In today's world, we don't just see people's lives. We scroll through them. Social media has turned success into a visual scoreboard. New homes. Perfect vacations. Designer labels. Lavish parties. It's a carefully curated illusion that rarely reveals the financial anxiety behind the lens. What you're really seeing is a highlight reel wrapped in debt. It's what I call Big Hat, No Cattle, a phrase that stuck with me from The Millionaire Next Door. It means pretending to have wealth while quietly drowning in the appearance of it. I know because I lived it.

The Lie I Bought Into

As a young Army lieutenant, I'd walk into the homes of senior officers and feel awe and envy. Their homes were filled with elegance and signs of status. I assumed that was what success looked like. And I wanted it, immediately. So, my ex-wife and I started buying the image. The best furniture. The upgraded car. The "right" clothes. All funded by credit cards and borrowed money. We weren't creating a life; we were purchasing an illusion.

At first, it felt exciting. But eventually, the debt became suffocating. The pressure, unbearable. We weren't chasing joy. We were chasing someone else's version of it, hoping to feel enough. That's the sinister power of comparison. It doesn't just affect what you buy. It affects why you buy. And if you're not careful, you'll trade your future for the appearance of success today.

Debt is painful. But comparison is the root disease. It convinces you to:

- Spend money you don't have
- Impress people who don't care
- At the expense of your peace, progress, and purpose

But here's the truth most people won't tell you:
Real wealth isn't loud. It's quiet. It's calm. It's disciplined.

The wealthiest, most grounded people I know aren't chasing likes or leveraging their lifestyle. They're building something sustainable and free. They're focused on legacy, not lifestyle. Freedom, not flash. When your decisions are driven by visuals instead of values, you will pay the price. Financially and emotionally. And trust me: the bill always comes due.

Choose Freedom Over Flash

So how do you break the cycle? You get brutally honest with yourself. You stop measuring your progress against someone else's projection. You decide that your future matters more than anyone else's opinion. And you remember: Every dollar spent to impress is a dollar taken from your dream. You don't need to look rich to become wealthy. You just need clarity, courage, and consistency. Don't buy the lifestyle lie. Build something better. Build something that feels free. Not just something that looks good.

The fastest way to sabotage your wealth is to try living someone else's life.

CONSIDER

Have you ever made a financial decision just to "keep up", even without realizing it?

Dig into the why behind your spending. That's where the transformation begins.

What triggers your sense of lack or inadequacy?

Social media? Family pressure? Cultural expectations? Identifying your triggers helps you take your power back.

Are your purchases aligned with your values, or are they someone else's idea of what success looks like?

Real alignment brings real peace.

ACTION

Define what financial freedom looks like for you.

Not your neighbor. Not your coworker. You. Let that vision guide your decisions.

Identify one status-symbol purchase this week and redirect that money to something that matters: savings, debt, or your dream.

Every choice is a step toward freedom.

DOABLE

Unfollow or mute one social media account that feeds insecurity or comparison.

Curate your environment. Protect your peace.

Chapter 23: Pay Creep: When More Money Still Isn't Enough

The Illusion of a Bigger Paycheck

You finally got the raise. The one you hoped for. The one you earned. You're making more money than ever before. But your savings haven't grown. Your debt hasn't shrunk. And your stress? Still quietly smoldering.

Welcome to pay creep. One of the most deceptive traps in personal finance. Pay creep happens when your income rises, but your lifestyle races to match it. Or worse, outruns it. Suddenly it's a bigger house, a newer car, trendier vacations, and more frequent dinners out. You don't feel like you're overspending because technically, you can afford it. But what you're really doing is treading water in nicer shoes.

I've watched it happen to people I respect. I've lived it myself. I'll never forget a colleague who earned a $10,000 raise and ended the year with less money in the bank. He leased a luxury car. Joined a high-end gym. Started dining out like he had no kitchen. He didn't notice the money slipping away until tax season exposed the truth. And that truth is this: more income doesn't automatically mean more wealth.

If you're not intentional, every new dollar will get absorbed by your new lifestyle. No matter how much you earn, it will never feel like enough because you're not using the raise to change your reality, just your surroundings.

The Turning Point: Automation

For me, the turning point came with one habit: automation.

I created a system that automatically routed a fixed percentage of my income to investing, saving, and giving before I ever saw it. That one strategy changed everything. It scaled with my income. And protected me from myself.

For example, I automated 5% of my income to flow directly into a traditional IRA. That percentage didn't change, but my salary did. So, my future kept growing, even when my spending temptations did too. My wealth started to build itself, quietly and steadily, because I had removed the friction. No discipline required. Just direction.

Automation was my safeguard. It ensured that my income increased my freedom, not just my lifestyle. It made building wealth the default, not the afterthought.

Progress or Performance?

Let me be clear: there's nothing wrong with enjoying the fruits of your labor. You should feel proud. You deserve comfort. The key is proportion. But if every raise leads to an equivalent lifestyle upgrade, you're not progressing, you're performing. And that performance has a cost. The hardest part? It doesn't feel like a problem. That's why pay creep is so dangerous. It masquerades as success.

The bigger house feels like growth. The new car feels like celebration. The international trip feels like reward. But too often, these upgrades delay your dreams instead of delivering them. Because wealth isn't built on income. It's built on what you keep.

If you don't give every dollar a job, it will find one you didn't choose. And chances are, that job won't serve your future.

A raise should increase your wealth, not just upgrade your lifestyle.

CONSIDER

When you received your last raise or bonus, where did that money go?

If you don't know, that's the first red flag. Unassigned money always disappears. Pay creep thrives in the absence of a plan.

Does your spending increase every time your income does?

If so, you're on a treadmill, not a track. It may feel like movement, but you're not getting anywhere. Strategy beats speed, every time.

Are you automating your finances to make wealth-building inevitable?

Hope is not a strategy. Automation removes the burden of discipline. It ensures your goals get paid before your impulses do.

ACTION

Write out an audit of your last three raises.

Compare the increase in income to your savings and investments. Did your wealth grow or your spending? This simple exercise builds powerful awareness.

DOABLE

This week, increase your automatic savings or investing transfer by even $25.

Don't wait for the next pay-raise. Start the habit now. Write down what you set up: Amount: __________ Account: __________ Start date: __________.

Chapter 24: Your Network Is Your Net Worth

Wealth Is a Team Sport

For years, I believed wealth was strictly a numbers game: earn more, save more, invest more. But the deeper I went into the journey, the more I realized something essential. Wealth is rarely built in isolation. Your relationships may be your most valuable asset. Here's what I've come to understand. It's not just who you know. It's who knows you, respects you, and is willing to speak your name in rooms you can't yet enter.

Your network is not a tally of business cards or LinkedIn connections. It's the ecosystem where your potential is either nurtured or neglected. I've lived this truth. Every meaningful leap I've made, personally or professionally, can be traced to someone who believed in me before I fully believed in myself. People who saw something in me and were willing to invest their time, trust, and credibility on my behalf.

A Relationship That Changed My Life

One of those people was President, Dr. Barbara McDonald.

In 2016, she hired me as Vice President of Finance at North Hennepin Community College. She mentored me, challenged me, and trusted me with real responsibility. I'll never forget the moment she told our leadership team she was a finalist for the presidency at the College of Saint Scholastica. I turned away, tears in my eyes. Not because I was sad, but because I was proud. I believed in her, just as she had believed in me. And when she got the job, she didn't stop investing in me. She recommended me to the president of Metropolitan State University. She later invited me to serve on the Board of Trustees at Saint Scholastica, where I've now served for more than three years.

That one relationship changed the entire trajectory of my career. But here's the lesson: that opportunity wasn't luck. It was the return on years of quiet excellence, service, and trust. I didn't just show up when I needed something. I showed up long before, with integrity and consistency. And when the door opened, I was ready. Strategic relationships aren't transactional. They're transformational.

Choose Your Rooms Carefully

But far too many of us stay in circles that keep us comfortable, not accountable. We invest time in people who drain us, doubt us, or distract us. If you're serious about growth, your relationships must reflect that seriousness. Your time, energy, and proximity are resources, and you must spend them like your future depends on it. Because it does.

There's a saying: if you're the smartest person in the room, you're in the wrong room. But I'd take it further: if you're the hungriest person in the room and no one else is striving, you'll eventually slow down to match the room. Your environment will either reinforce your ambition or erode it.

That's why I started pursuing new rooms. I've joined communities, attended conferences, and served alongside leaders I admire. Every step into a new circle stretched me. And while I worked on my network, I also worked on myself. Because you can't ask people to invest in a version of you that doesn't exist yet.

Jim Rohn once said, "Work on your job, you make a living. Work on yourself, you make a fortune." So, I study mentors, even those I haven't met, through books, podcasts, conversations, and reflection. I call them my Master Mentors. And that inner work is what makes me someone worth investing in.

Here's the truth: social capital can open more doors than financial capital. A single introduction can unlock what years of grinding couldn't. But no one opens doors for someone they don't trust. So, ask yourself: are you building trust before you ask for opportunity?

I've met mentors in places I didn't expect. On flights. At the gym. Officiating youth sports. But none of those moments would've mattered if I wasn't ready to connect: mentally, emotionally, and spiritually. Even JESUS built a circle before launching HIS mission. So why do we think we can do this alone? Your future is being shaped by the five people you give the most of your time to. Are they sharpening your vision, or slowly dulling it?

Relationships are the real currency of life. And the Return On Investment (ROI) becomes exponential when relationships are rooted in integrity, generosity, and shared purpose.

Let me be clear: I'm not talking about using people. I'm talking about building *with* people. There's a difference. When your vision is clear and your values are strong, the right relationships become force multipliers. Who are you becoming? And who are you walking with? Because those answers will tell you exactly where you're headed.

Your future will rise or fall to the level of the people you surround yourself with.

CONSIDER

Think about the five people you spend the most time with. How are they shaping your mindset and money habits?

Your circle sets your standard. Proximity determines possibility.

Are you choosing growth over comfort when it comes to your relationships?

Stagnant company caps potential. Get in the rooms where your next level is the norm, not the exception.

What does your current network believe about wealth, generosity, and growth?

Are they reinforcing your values or quietly rewriting them? Align your circle with your goals, or your goals will adapt to your circle.

ACTION

List three people you admire and want to learn from.

Reach out to one this week. The conversation doesn't have to be perfect, just intentional. Momentum follows courage.

DOABLE

Join one new community or event this month that aligns with your future.

Exposure breeds expansion. And every new room increases the odds of your next breakthrough.

Chapter 25: Entrepreneurship: Creating Instead of Chasing Opportunities

The Entrepreneur I Didn't Recognize

For a long time, I didn't see myself as an entrepreneur. That title felt like it belonged to someone else. Someone with an MBA, a tech startup, or a line of venture capital waiting in the wings. I didn't come from that world. I came from the world of PO. Not just poor, but PO. We didn't have investments or incubators. We had ingenuity. And survival taught us the earliest lessons in business: supply and demand, customer service, and grit. I just didn't know it was entrepreneurship yet.

Selling candy at school. Mowing lawns in the summer. Flipping sneakers. That was us creating value with whatever we had. No marketing strategy. No business loan. Just hustle. That's the raw version of entrepreneurship. Before the boardroom. Before the business card.

Looking back, I realize now that the greatest thing poverty taught me wasn't how to stretch a dollar. It was how to create one. Entrepreneurs don't wait. They act. They look at a problem and ask, "What can I build that solves this?" They turn ideas into income and passion into platforms. They own their path instead of asking for a seat at someone else's table.

It wasn't until I started Be the Best Foundation that I began to see myself through that lens. And since then, I've had a front-row seat to people who turned nothing into something. With faith, resilience, and audacity.

Entrepreneurship in Action

Take Isaiah. I met him after a high school talk in the Twin Cities. He introduced himself with confidence and said, "I'm an entrepreneur. I run a car detailing business." I loved that energy. I told him, "Perfect. I want you to detail my car." He followed me out, sized up the vehicle, and said with a smile, "$60. Your car is already immaculate." I laughed. He was honest, sharp, and professional. I paid him $100, not just for the detail, but for his excellence. Then I told my network. He kept showing up, and his name kept spreading. That's entrepreneurship. No ad spends. Just integrity and delivery.

We live in a time when you can launch a brand with a smartphone and a skill. The problem isn't lack of opportunity. It's hesitation. It's fear disguised as perfectionism. Most people aren't waiting for a better plan, they're waiting to feel "ready." Entrepreneurship isn't about being ready. It's about being willing.

Start with what's in your hands. A skill. A story. A service. Package it. Price it. Promote it. Then deliver it well. That's how businesses are born. And don't think you have to do it alone.

One of the most strategic moves you can make as an entrepreneur is to build your circle: mentors, collaborators, believers. Success accelerates when you stop trying to do everything yourself. Community builds capacity.

Create Your Own Lane

And one of the biggest reasons to pursue entrepreneurship, especially if you've ever been overlooked, underestimated, or systemically shut out, is control. Control over your time. Your income. Your mission. Your impact.

No gatekeeper can block your purpose when you create your own lane.

I think of Kevin Da Barbr, someone I met in 2017. He told me he dreamed of owning a barbershop that wasn't just a place for haircuts, but a cultural hub for the community. I watched him grind for years, shop to shop, staying committed to the dream. He didn't have overnight success. He had daily belief! Today, he's the proud owner of Culture Hip Hop Barbershop in

Brooklyn Center, Minnesota and it has the most affirming energy I've ever experienced in a barbershop. What started as a vision is now his everyday reality. That's the power of persistence. That's what happens when you stay in the fight.

Entrepreneurship doesn't just build income. It builds character. It demands consistency. It requires self-trust. It tests your capacity for rejection, resilience, and reinvention. And even if you love your 9-to-5, there's wisdom in owning something of your own. A business, a brand, a side hustle. It's not just about multiple streams of income; it's about multiple streams of security.

You were not created to bury your gifts. You were created to build with them.

Opportunities rarely appear fully formed.
Entrepreneurs build them.

CONSIDER

Have you counted yourself out of entrepreneurship before ever giving yourself a chance?

You don't need a perfect plan to start. You need the courage to explore. You may already have the skills, the story, and the solution someone is waiting for.

How would your life change if just one of your passions became profitable?

When your income aligns with your energy, something shifts. You become more fulfilled, more focused, and freer.

ACTION

Pick the idea that excites you most. Then answer three questions:

(1) What problem does it solve?

(2) Who needs it?

(3) How could you get paid for it? That's your starting point. It doesn't have to be perfect. Just write it down.

DOABLE

This week, take one concrete step toward the idea you outlined. Research it, talk to someone who does it, or test it with one person.

Most success stories don't begin with clarity. They begin with courage. Let their story fuel yours.

Chapter 26: Staying Free: Protecting Your Progress Once You're Unshackled

Freedom Requires Protection

Getting out of financial bondage is a breakthrough. Staying out is a battle. Freedom doesn't sustain itself. It must be guarded strategically, intentionally, and with humility. Because what once shackled you, whether debt, distraction, or denial, has a way of returning quietly. Old habits don't need permission to come back. They just need your guard to be down.

Complacency is not rest. It's regression. And if you're not vigilant, you'll look up and realize you've rebuilt the same prison you once escaped, only with nicer furniture. I've been there. The temptation to "reward yourself" can feel like healing. But it can be sabotage in disguise. The voice that says "just this once" isn't always loud. Sometimes it sounds like comfort. Like celebration. Like self-care. But anything that risks your peace of mind for a fleeting high is not freedom. It's a trade, and not a good one. So how do you protect your freedom? You build a system around it.

Habits Protect Your Freedom

Your locks are your habits: budgeting, saving, automating, and delaying gratification. These aren't just financial tools. They're emotional anchors. They remind you who you are now and who you never want to be again.

And here's the truth that's hard to admit: even after you've made it out, you'll still feel the pull to go back. Not to debt, necessarily, but to the illusion of ease. To perform. To impress. To keep up. But real wealth doesn't need to be seen. It needs to be stewarded. That's why the people who are truly wealthy often look like they aren't. They've chosen peace over performance. Discipline over dopamine.

Reminders—Systems Protect Your Freedom

The biggest post-freedom threat? Lifestyle creep. Again, it's seductive, disguised as growth, masked as success. But if your expenses rise as fast as your income, you're not building wealth. You're building a fancier form of dependence. Don't confuse earning more with permission to spend more. Create space between income and lifestyle. That gap is where true freedom lives.

Reminder! Emotions are part of this equation too. Joy, stress, loss, boredom. They all affect how we spend. I've bought things I didn't need just to avoid feelings I didn't want to face. That's why you need guardrails, not just goals. Systems that work even when your willpower doesn't.

Automate what matters. Save without thinking. Invest on schedule. Pay your bills before your desires. Because at your lowest moments, you won't rise to the level of your aspirations. You will fall to the level of your systems.

People Protect Your Freedom

Also, be honest about your circle. You don't need cheerleaders. You need challengers. People who remind you of your "why" when you begin to drift. People who are willing to ask hard questions, not because they doubt you, but because they care enough to protect your progress.

For me, that person has long been my best friend, Will (Big Money). His quiet discipline has been a constant reminder that success is not about hype. It is about consistency. When I needed perspective, he gave it. When I needed encouragement, he offered it without hesitation. Accountability like that is priceless. Sometimes the greatest gift someone can give you is the courage to remind you who you said you wanted to become.

Freedom is easier to protect when someone else can see your blind spots. If you want to stay free, keep learning. Don't just grow your bank account. Grow your mindset. Upgrade your financial literacy, emotional maturity, and relational accountability. The person who built your freedom isn't enough to sustain it. You'll need to become someone new again and again. Stay humble. Stay hungry. But don't stay isolated.

Create an emergency plan. Not out of fear, but out of wisdom. Life will come for you. Unexpected job loss, medical bills, family emergencies. Your ability to respond instead of react will protect the progress you've made.

And above all, stay connected. Freedom isn't a solo sport. Whether it's your partner, a friend, or a mentor. Find someone who knows your goals and won't let you drift. You don't need someone perfect. Just someone honest. Sometimes the most strategic move you can make is to admit: "I can't do this alone."

Financial freedom is not a destination. It is a discipline you protect every day.

CONSIDER

Who calls you out when your financial behavior doesn't align with your values?
If the answer is no one, what does that cost you?"

What is the one financial habit that, if you stopped doing it, would put everything you've built at risk?
Are you still doing it?

ACTION

Create a protection plan, step by step.
Not to be paranoid, but to be prepared. Emergencies are inevitable. Panic is optional.

Recommit to one core habit that helped you get debt-free.
Whether that's meal planning, weekly budget check-ins, or automatic savings transfers. Strength lives in repetition.

DOABLE

Do you have an accountability partner?
If yes, reach out to them to share where you are, where you're headed, and ask for honest feedback. Your vulnerability builds their trust and your momentum.

Chapter 27: Faith in the Financial Fight

Faith and finances collide in ways most people never talk about. When you're behind on bills, drowning in debt, or lying awake at night wondering how to keep going, it's not just a numbers problem. It's a test of belief. A test of identity. A test of endurance. And sometimes, the greatest battles in your financial life aren't fought in your bank account. They're fought in your spirit.

I've lived that test. As you know, earlier in my journey I found myself staring at nearly $100,000 in debt. My young family depended on me, and my military paycheck stretched thinner than our faith some days. We moved from base to base, carrying not just bags, but the weight of uncertainty. Every spreadsheet said we wouldn't make it. But somehow, faith kept whispering: "Keep going."

I didn't feel strong. I felt exhausted and mostly ashamed. But I showed up anyway. Because when everything in my life felt unstable, faith became the one thing I could stand on. Not faith as a cliché, but faith as a quiet commitment to believe GOD was still working, even when I couldn't see the outcome.

Faith and Strategy Work Together

Here's what I've learned: faith and strategy aren't opposites. They're partners. Faith without a plan leads to frustration. And strategy without faith leads to burnout. But together? They're powerful.

I used to think budgeting was about math. But it's just as much about mindset. It's spiritual discipline. A way to steward what GOD has given and align my resources with my purpose. Every dollar became a declaration: “I believe there’s more coming. I believe I can break this cycle. I believe I’m building something bigger than a balance sheet.”

Too often, we treat GOD like HE only belongs in church, not in our checking accounts. But HE cares about both. HE speaks through both. I stopped seeing tithing as a burden and started seeing it as a trust exercise. When I gave, even when it was uncomfortable, it rewired my priorities. It reminded me that provision doesn’t come from a paycheck alone. It comes from purpose.

The Bible became my financial coach. Proverbs taught me diligence, generosity, and patience. JESUS warned about money not to shame us, but to shape us. HE knew how easily we confuse wealth with worth. Some of my biggest breakthroughs didn’t come from books. They came from rock-bottom prayers. The ones I prayed through tears. Through fear. Through fatigue. And over time, I saw the fruit. Not always more money, but more wisdom. More peace. More alignment. And eventually, more overflow.

Faith steadied me when job uncertainty hit. When the market dipped. When unexpected bills arrived. Faith didn’t stop the storm, but it anchored me in the middle of it. It reminded me: I’m not building just for today. I’m building something eternal. Something generational. And here's the truth: I believe that GOD doesn’t necessarily bless perfection. HE blesses progress. HE honors intentionality. Stewardship. Obedience. Not because HE needs it, but because we do. Faith stretches our vision beyond just getting by. It pushes us to believe we’re called not just to survive but to build.

When the Storm Hits

So, if you’re in the middle of your own financial storm, here’s what I want to say to you: you’re not behind. You’re being prepared. The habits you form now, the prayers you pray now, the seeds you plant now, will become the freedom you walk in later. Faith isn't just your lifeline. It's the launchpad for everything you're about to build.

Your financial life is not just a test of knowledge. It is a test of faith.

CONSIDER

Have you invited GOD into your financial life or have you been carrying it all alone?

What might change if you surrendered both your goals and your fears?

When unexpected expenses or setbacks arise, how do you respond?

Panic and retreat, or pause and pray? Your reaction reveals your foundation. Build it wisely.

Are you building a financial future rooted in fear or anchored in faith?

One leaves you striving. The other frees you to build, give, and live with confidence.

ACTION

Write a prayer over your financial life.

Include three things: what you are surrendering to GOD, what you are trusting HIM for, and what you are building toward. Revisit it every week.

Keep a record of answered prayers alongside your budget.

When GOD moves, write it down. Faith grows when you can look back and see what GOD has done, not just in your bank account, but in your character.

DOABLE

Memorize one scripture this month about stewardship, provision, or diligence.

Let it be your anchor when fear rises and your fuel when motivation fades.

Chapter 28: Mastering Money Conversations in Relationships

Money is never just about dollars and cents. In relationships, it's about trust, priorities, pain, and power. And when it goes unspoken, it rarely stays unproblematic. If we're honest, many of us were never taught how to talk about money, especially with the people we love most. But if you want lasting connection and shared purpose, you must learn.

For years, I avoided the hard money talks. Not because I didn't care, but because I carried shame. I didn't want to expose how messy things were. My ex-wife and I came from similar backgrounds, both raised in households that lacked money and, even more importantly, lacked healthy money habits. We were united by struggle but not always aligned in strategy. Over time, that silence turned into stress, judgment, and distance.

Looking back, I realized we weren't necessarily wrong in how we each approached money. We just weren't talking about it. And without communication, tension brewed. When the penny-stock loss I mentioned earlier happened, it wasn't just a financial blow. It became a breaking point. That moment forced me to confront my ego, my fear, and my unwillingness to be fully transparent. It taught me that you cannot build trust on half-truths. In many ways it fractured us, but a healing process also began in me that continues to this day.

Money Conversations Build Trust

In any relationship, romantic, familial, or business, money conversations aren't optional. They're essential. Alignment doesn't happen by accident; it's built through honesty, repetition, and deep listening. If you're not equally yoked in how you see, spend, and save money, the cracks will show. Love can't patch over financial misalignment forever.

I used to think vulnerability with money made me weak. Now I know it makes me stronger. It invites collaboration. It creates space for accountability. And it deepens intimacy, not just in marriage, but in parenting, friendships, and business partnerships too.

Business Relationships Raise the Stakes

Business partnerships taught me some of the same lessons, but the stakes were often higher.

When money and friendship mix, assumptions become dangerous. One partner may think profits should be reinvested. Another may expect distributions. One person might treat the venture like a side project while the other treats it like their livelihood. If those expectations are never discussed, resentment quietly grows.

I've learned that strong business relationships don't rely on trust alone. They rely on clarity. Clear roles. Clear responsibilities. Clear expectations about money.

Before entering any financial partnership, ask the questions most people avoid:

- Who controls financial decisions?
- How are profits distributed?
- What happens if one partner wants out?
- What happens if the business struggles?
- What happens if one partner contributes more than the other?

Those conversations can feel uncomfortable at first. But avoiding them is far more uncomfortable later. In business, written agreements are not signs of distrust. They are signs of wisdom. Contracts don't damage relationships; they protect them. The healthiest partnerships I've seen share three traits:

Transparency. Accountability. Communication.

Partners review numbers together. They talk through problems early. And they make decisions based on long-term vision, not short-term emotion.

When money is involved, silence can become the most expensive mistake of all. Unspoken assumptions quietly sabotage relationships. One unmet expectation, one misunderstood agreement, and everything can fall apart. That is why I now insist on written clarity, recurring check-ins, and honest conversations before things go sideways.

And here's what I've learned: good money communication isn't about confrontation. It's about curiosity. Instead of leading with "Why did you do that?" try, "What's your approach to money and where did that come from?" The tone changes everything. Empathy changes everything.

Money talks are also emotional because they're rarely just about money. They're about how we define security. What we fear. What we hope for. What we were taught and what we were trying to unlearn. So be gentle with yourself and with others. The goal isn't perfection. It's progress, partnership, and peace.

Don't wait until a crisis forces the conversation. Schedule the talks. Make them normal. Celebrate the wins. Talk through the setbacks. If you want to build anything lasting, with your spouse, kids, or business partners, you must build on financial truth.

If it's been a point of conflict, there's no shame in seeking help. A third-party voice can often guide the conversation when it's too charged to manage alone. The bravest thing you can do isn't avoid the conversation, it's start it. Financial trust is built the same way wealth is built through consistency over time.

Silence about money doesn't protect relationships. It slowly erodes them.

CONSIDER

Is there something about your money that your partner or family doesn't know?

What are you afraid would happen if they did?

What did you learn about money from watching the adults around you growing up? How does that show up in how you talk or don't talk about money with the people you love now?

Awareness is the first step to rewriting the script.

ACTION

Initiate a financial conversation with someone close to you. Spouse, partner, child, or business colleague.

Don't wait for conflict. Lead with love and curiosity.

Take this action a step further: write down three shared financial goals.

Review them monthly. Progress isn't just about income. It's about alignment, discipline, and shared direction.

DOABLE

Schedule a 30-minute "Money Clarity Conversation" this week with someone important in your life.

Use three questions:

> What does financial security look like to you?
>
> What money habits from childhood still influence you today?
>
> What financial goal should we pursue together in the next 12 months?

Write down the answers.

Chapter 29: From Success to Significance

When Success Stops Being Enough

There comes a point in every transformation journey when the metrics change. When the numbers in your account don't hit the same as the impact in someone else's life. When success no longer feels like the finish line, but the foundation.

The Question That Changes Everything

I've tasted success. I've crushed goals, climbed out of debt, hit financial milestones I once thought were impossible. And for a while, that was enough. The validation. The pride. The freedom. But eventually, I started asking a deeper question: What am I building this for? And that question opened the door to something greater: significance.

Success is about what you earn. Significance is about who you serve. It's when your story becomes someone else's survival guide. When your wins make the road smoother for those coming behind you.

Turning Success Into Service

I didn't get here on my own. And I don't want the next generation to start where I started. That's why I founded Be the Best Foundation, to turn success into service. To mentor, to educate, to provide a blueprint that I never had. It wasn't about creating a brand. It was about creating a bridge.

Significance doesn't require millions. It requires intention. It asks you to look at what you've been through and what you've overcome, and ask, "How can this help someone else?" It calls you to turn pain into purpose, and lessons into leadership.

One of the most humbling and honoring moments in my journey is seeing a young person light up when they realize they matter. When they see themselves differently because you showed up. That moment? It's worth more than any paycheck or portfolio gain. That moment is why I keep going.

The world teaches us to chase success, titles, things, status. But real legacy lives in how we show up for others. In the tables we build. In the stories we share. In the wisdom we pass down, not to impress, but to equip.

Legacy Is Built Daily

I used to think legacy started later in life. I was wrong. It starts now. With how you speak to your kids. With how you mentor. With how you spend your time, your talent, your resources. Legacy is built in daily decisions. Most of them quiet, unseen, and uncelebrated.

The Ripple Effect

Success brought me freedom. But significance brings me peace. Knowing that what I've been through wasn't wasted, and is being repurposed to lift others, is the most fulfilling part of this journey. Not the numbers. Not the accolades. The ripple effect.

So if you're striving right now, keep going. But know this: when you reach your goals, don't stop there. Use your success to spark someone else's. Use your platform to pull others forward. Use your voice to make sure someone else doesn't stay stuck in silence.

Because the truth is, we don't rise just to rise. We rise to reach. To lift. To teach. To serve. That's not just how you live ***Unshackled***. That's how you make sure others find their freedom too. That's legacy. That's significance.

Success changes your life. Significance changes other people's lives.

CONSIDER

How has your definition of success changed as you've grown?

Are your current goals aligned with your purpose, or are you still chasing something that used to matter but no longer does?

What part of your story could serve someone else?

What have you learned the hard way that could become someone else's breakthrough?

Are you living like your legacy starts now or like it's something you'll figure out later?

What small, consistent actions can you take today to live a life that echoes?

ACTION

Choose one life lesson from your journey and write about it. Whether to your child, a mentee, or your community, sharing your wisdom multiplies your impact and cements your significance.

DOABLE

Identify one person you can lift, mentor, or support this month. Send the text. Make the call. Open the door. Your time and presence may be the spark they've needed for a long time.

Chapter 30: Teach the Next Generation

Wealth That Outlives You

True wealth isn't just about what you accumulate. It's about what you pass on. Not just to your children, but to your community. To your culture. To the world. For me, the most powerful return on investment isn't measured in dollars. It's measured in lives changed.

I wasn't raised with financial wisdom at the dinner table. I had to fight for what I know now through trial, error, and a whole lot of humility. That's exactly why I'm so committed to teaching the next generation. Because no one should have to stumble their way to financial truth if someone else has already walked the road.

A Generation Searching for Guidance

Since retiring from corporate America, I've spoken to hundreds of teens on stages, in barbershops, gyms, classrooms, wherever they gather. And every time, I'm reminded: they're hungry. Not just for information, but for transformation. They want to learn. They just need someone to show up.

The Financial Literacy Crisis

Why do I pour so much into this? Because the numbers break my heart. Median Black household wealth is a tenth of that of White households. Latino households face similar barriers, including limited access, less support, less education. Only 28% of Black Americans own stock. Only 17 states require financial literacy in school. And nearly half of Gen Z says they're stressed about money but don't feel prepared to handle it.

That's not a statistic. It's a crisis. And we can't fix it with silence.

When I speak to students, I don't sugarcoat. I tell them the truth. Most Americans will rely heavily on Social Security and limited savings to survive in retirement. Only a small percentage achieve true financial freedom. So, I ask them, "Who wants to be a millionaire?" Hands go up. "Now who's willing to act like one today because only about 5% achieve true financial freedom. That's the harder question. Because it takes more than desire. It takes mindset, discipline, and structure.

The Lessons They Deserve to Hear

That's why I teach them what I wish someone had told me:
- Avoid debt traps at all costs.
- Start investing early. Even if it's just $25/month.
- Let your money grow while you sleep.
- Live below your means. Stay humble. Stay hungry.
- Learn. Apply. Repeat.

But more than that, I try to model it. Because they might forget my words, but they won't forget how I made them feel: seen, capable, and worthy of financial success.

This chapter isn't about theory. It's about legacy. Because your legacy isn't what you leave for the next generation. It's what you leave in them. Teach boldly. Share generously. Let your wisdom ripple across decades.

You Now Carry the Torch

You've made it this far in the book for a reason. By now, you understand the fundamentals of building wealth. You've learned about mindset, discipline, saving, investing, and legacy. These aren't just financial concepts anymore. They're tools. And tools aren't meant to sit on a shelf. They're meant to be used.

The next generation doesn't just need another motivational speech. They need someone who can show them the path. Now you can. You understand how money works. You understand how discipline compounds. You understand how small decisions shape entire futures. That means you now carry something powerful: financial wisdom earned through experience.

Wisdom that isn't shared eventually disappears. So, pass it forward. Teach a child. Mentor a student. Have conversations most families avoid. Because when knowledge moves from one generation to the next, entire family trees change. Help them dream generously and plan practically

Dream Generously. Plan Practically.

One of my favorite questions to ask a young person is simple: **"What would you give if money wasn't an issue?"** At first, they usually laugh. Then they start dreaming. Helping family. Building schools. Supporting charities. Changing their community. That moment matters. Because generosity reveals purpose. But dreaming alone isn't enough. Once they share their vision, I ask the follow-up question:

"What kind of life would you need to build to make that possible?"

That's when the lesson begins. You show them that generosity is powered by discipline. That wealth isn't just about buying things. It's about creating the ability to bless others. Dream generously. Plan practically. That's how legacies begin. The greatest wealth you will ever create isn't in your bank account. It's in the minds you inspire.

Financial freedom becomes legacy the moment you teach someone else how to achieve it.

CONSIDER

Who poured financial wisdom into you, and who are you pouring into now?

Maybe you didn't grow up learning about money. That cycle ends with you. Every truth you share is a seed planted for their future harvest.

Think about the young people in your life right now. Do they know how to handle money? Do they understand that how you think about money matters just as much as how much you earn?
Money follows mindset. Without belief, knowledge has no power. Model the confidence, discipline, and long-term thinking they need to carry forward.

ACTION

Write down three things you wish someone had taught you about money before you had to learn them the hard way.
Those lessons are your gifts to someone else.

Take a step farther: Choose one of the life lessons from your journey and pass it on.
Whether to your child, niece, nephew, mentee, or your community. Sharing your wisdom multiplies your impact and cements your significance.

DOABLE

Have a 10-minute money conversation with a young person this week.
Ask them three questions:
What do you want your life to look like when you're older?
What would you give to others if money wasn't an issue?
What money habits do you think people need to succeed?

Listen carefully. Then share one lesson you learned the hard way. Simple conversations like this can change the direction of someone's entire financial life.

Chapter 31: Conclusion: The Unshackled Life

Financial freedom begins with knowledge. The Unshackled Life begins with action.

If you've made it this far, you didn't just read a book. You walked through a transformation. You walked through struggle and strategy. Through fear and faith. Through mistakes, discipline, and growth. You didn't just learn about money. You learned how to change the trajectory of your life.

This journey began with a boy from Mississippi who grew up "PO." Not poor. Just starting with very little. And from that beginning came a simple realization that shaped everything that followed:

Where you start does not determine where you finish.

What You've Learned

Throughout this book, we've dismantled the chains that keep people financially trapped. First, we confronted mindset. You learned that wealth begins in the mind long before it appears in a bank account. Your beliefs about money, discipline, and possibility shape every financial outcome that follows. If your thinking remains shackled, your finances will be too.

Then we addressed the fundamentals. You learned how to budget with intention, destroy destructive debt, protect your credit score, and build the saving habits that create financial stability. These aren't glamorous steps, but they are the foundation of every strong financial life.

From there, we moved into building wealth. You discovered the extraordinary power of compound interest, the discipline of investing consistently, and the quiet advantage of strategies like dollar-cost averaging. You learned that wealth isn't built through luck or timing. It's built through patience, consistency, and time.

You also learned to protect what you build. Taxes, insurance, estate planning, and financial protection aren't just paperwork. They are armor. Because building wealth without protecting it leaves everything vulnerable. But wealth is about more than numbers.

You explored the psychology of money and the emotional patterns that shape financial behavior. You confronted comparison, lifestyle inflation, and the subtle ways success can be quietly sabotaged.

You learned that relationships matter too. Your network shapes your net worth. Your conversations about money shape the strength of your partnerships. Transparency, trust, and alignment determine whether wealth builds unity or conflict.

You discovered that ownership matters. Entrepreneurship, multiple income streams, and financial independence all create options. Options to live life on your own terms rather than someone else's timetable.

And finally, we talked about the purpose behind it all. Legacy. Significance. Teaching the next generation. Because true wealth isn't measured by what you accumulate. It's measured by what you multiply in the lives of others. That's the real goal. Not just financial success. But a life that creates opportunity, wisdom, and freedom for generations to come.

The Unshackled Life

And now, here you stand. At the doorway to what I call **The Unshackled Life.** The Unshackled Life isn't about luxury. It's about freedom. Freedom from destructive debt. Freedom from paycheck-to-paycheck stress. Freedom from comparison and consumer traps. Freedom to give generously. Freedom to invest in the future. Freedom to live according to purpose rather than pressure. Everything you need to build an Unshackled life is now in your hands.

Your Next Step

But here is the truth that must be said clearly: Knowledge alone will not change your life. **Action** will. You now have the tools. You understand the systems. You have seen the blueprint. But the miracle is not in the reading. As Jim Rohn famously said, "The miracle is in the labor."

Just as a mother labors to bring new life into the world, your effort, your discipline, your consistency, and your decisions will give birth to a new financial life. And that labor begins today.
Not next year.
Not when things feel easier. Not when circumstances are perfect.
It begins now.

Work like it all depends on you. Believe like it all depends on GOD.

I once heard a truth that changed my life:

"If I row the boat, GOD will steer. But GOD said HE will not row."

In other words, the effort is ours. But the direction is HIS. If we show up with discipline, faith, and integrity, HE can guide us toward purposes far greater than we imagined.

Oprah once said she asked GOD to reveal the dreams HE had for her life. That idea struck me deeply. I began praying those same words. And when you begin asking GOD to show you what HE sees in you, something powerful happens. You stop thinking small. You stop settling. You stop living according to fear. Instead, you begin rowing that boat every single day with purpose, with clarity, and with joy. So, here is your final charge.

📖 Re-read what matters.
✏️ Highlight what challenges you.
💬 Teach what you've learned.
✴️ Live what you believe.

Let your copy of this book become worn and marked up. Dog-eared pages. Highlighted lessons. Notes in the margins. Let it show that you didn't simply read *Unshackled.* **You lived it.** Because freedom is not a destination. It's a lifestyle. And from this moment forward, you don't just hope for a better future. **You build it.** One decision at a time. One disciplined habit at a time. One courageous conversation at a time. One legacy-shaping action at a time. So go build the life you were meant to live. Go lead with wisdom. Go give with generosity. Go! Walk in purpose. And above all, Go live...

Unshackled.

Because somewhere right now, someone is standing exactly where you once stood. Confused, overwhelmed, and wondering if financial freedom is even possible. Let your life become proof that it is.

Your Life Starts Now!

You didn't just finish a book. You just crossed a line that most people never reach. Most people talk about changing their financial life. Very few commit to doing it. You just spent hours learning how wealth actually works. How discipline builds freedom. How patience multiplies money. How mindset shapes destiny. But the truth is simple: Nothing in this book matters unless you act on it. Not tomorrow. Not someday. Now.

You already know enough to change your life.

You know how to:

- Destroy debt
- Build savings
- Invest consistently
- Protect your assets
- Multiply your income
- Build legacy

The blueprint is no longer hidden from you. The only question left is: Will you live it? The Unshackled life isn't reserved for the lucky. It belongs to the disciplined. So, from this moment forward: Choose discipline over distraction. Choose patience over hype. Choose ownership over excuses. And watch what happens to your life.

Now It's Your Turn

You've read the words. You've heard the stories. You've gathered the blueprint. But now it is time to build. **Unshackled** was never meant to sit quietly on a bookshelf. It was written to ignite action. So, before you turn the final page, pause and declare this truth over yourself:

"I am not who I was.

I am becoming who I was created to be."

Your next chapter will not be written in ink. It will be written in discipline. In courage. In consistent action. The habits you build today will shape the legacy you leave tomorrow. So, pick up the pen. Pick up the tools. Start building the life you were meant to live. And when your story begins to shift, big or small, I want to hear about it.

Email us at info@stephenekent.com and share how you have been **Unshackled**.

Your breakthrough might inspire the next reader to believe again. It may even be featured in a future edition of this book. Because this isn't just a book. It's a movement. And now you're a part of it.

THE UNSHACKLED PLEDGE

My Declaration of Discipline, Wealth, and Legacy

I take full ownership of my financial future.

I live by discipline, budget with wisdom, and spend intentionally

I reject the traps of comparison, debt, and distraction.

I save with purpose and invest with patience.

I build wealth steadily, give generously, and teach the next generation.

I live **Unshackled.**

Signed: ________________________________

Date: ________________________________

Share This Book

If this book helped you see money differently, share it with someone who needs it. Financial literacy spreads one conversation at a time. Leave a review. Recommend it to a friend. Start a discussion. Because when one life changes, an entire family tree can change.

Appendix A: Practical Financial Tools

Free Annual Credit Report

Federal law allows one free credit report each year from Experian, Equifax, and TransUnion.

Visit: https://www.annualcreditreport.com

Free Credit Score Monitoring

Many credit card companies provide free credit score monitoring for customers.

Debt Snowball vs. Avalanche

Snowball Method – Pay smallest debt first to build motivation.

Avalanche Method – Pay highest interest rate first to minimize cost.

Appendix B: Recommended Reading

Financial Strategy

• Rich Dad, Poor Dad – Robert Kiyosaki

• The Millionaire Next Door – Thomas J. Stanley & William D. Danko

• The Automatic Millionaire – David Bach

• The Compound Effect – Darren Hardy

• Die With Zero – Bill Perkins

• Get Good with Money – Tiffany Aliche

• The Wealth Decision – Dominique Broadway

Mindset & Personal Development

• The Magic of Thinking Big – David J. Schwartz

• Secrets of the Millionaire Mind – T. Harv Eker

• The Science of Getting Rich – Wallace D. Wattles

• The Power of Positive Thinking – Norman Vincent Peale

• The Neville Collection – Neville Goddard

• The Success Principles – Jack Canfield

Appendix C: My Daily Discipline Declaration/Audible Confession

This is my Bible.

I AM who it says I AM.

I do what it says I can do.

I can be who it says I can be.

I AM the head and not the tail.

I AM above only and not beneath.

I AM blessed in the city and blessed in the field.

I AM blessed going in and blessed going out.

I will meditate on this book of the law, day and night.

So that I might be careful to do all that is written in it.

And I will be prosperous and have good success.

Everything I touch prospers.

My mind and body prosper. My spirit and soul prosper.

My relationships and health prosper.

My finances and vision prosper.

I AM slow to talk and quick to listen,

Because I AM searching for wisdom.
I will continually train my mind because, thoughts lead to feelings,

Feelings lead to emotions; emotions lead to attitude and

Attitude is everything.

I AM as I thinketh, so therefore, I think GODly.

I will dream big dreams,

I shall attain my riches for YOUR glory.

I can do all things through CHRIST who strengthens me.

I AM more than a conqueror, and I am convinced that nothing shall

Separate me from the love of GOD thru CHRIST JESUS my LORD.

Surely goodness and mercy shall follow me all the days of my life.

And I will dwell in the house of the LORD forever.

And by HIS stripes I AM healed. And if GOD is for me, who can be against me?

In JESUS' name.

Amen.

Glossary of Key Financial Terms

Asset

Anything of value you own that can produce income or appreciate in value, such as investments, real estate, or businesses.

Bear Market

A prolonged period when stock prices decline, typically defined as a drop of 20% or more from recent highs.

Bull Market

A period when stock prices are rising and investor confidence is strong.

Capital Gains

Profit from the sale of an asset such as stocks or real estate.

Compound Interest

Interest calculated on both the original principal and the accumulated interest from previous periods.

Credit Score

A numerical representation of your creditworthiness based on borrowing and repayment history.

Credit Utilization

The percentage of your available credit that you are currently using.

Delayed Gratification

The ability to resist immediate rewards in favor of larger, long-term benefits. Delayed gratification is a core trait of disciplined investors and wealth builders, allowing small sacrifices today to produce greater financial freedom in the future.

Diversification

Spreading investments across multiple assets to reduce risk.

Dollar Cost Averaging (DCA)

An investment strategy that involves investing a fixed amount of money at regular intervals regardless of market conditions.

ETF (Exchange-Traded Fund)

A basket of securities such as stocks or bonds that trades on an exchange like a stock.

Emergency Fund

Savings set aside to cover unexpected expenses such as medical bills, job loss, or urgent repairs.

FICO Score

A widely used credit score developed by Fair Isaac Corporation, typically ranging from 300 to 850.

Financial Independence

The point at which your investments and passive income can support your lifestyle without requiring employment income.

Index Fund

An investment fund designed to track a market index such as the S&P 500.

Inflation

The gradual increase in prices over time that reduces the purchasing power of money.

Lifestyle Inflation

The gradual increase in spending that often occurs as income rises. Instead of building wealth, higher earnings are absorbed by larger homes, nicer cars, and upgraded lifestyles. When lifestyle inflation goes unchecked, it prevents savings and investing from growing despite increased income.

Liquidity

How quickly an asset can be converted into cash without significantly affecting its value.

Market Volatility

The degree to which investment prices move up and down over time.

Mutual Fund

An investment vehicle made up of a pool of money collected from many investors to purchase securities.

Net Worth

The total value of all assets owned minus all liabilities owed.

Passive Income

Income earned with minimal ongoing effort, such as dividends, rental income, or royalties.

Portfolio

The collection of investments owned by an individual or institution.

Risk Tolerance

An investor's ability and willingness to endure fluctuations in the value of their investments.

Roth IRA

A retirement account funded with after-tax dollars that allows tax-free withdrawals in retirement.

Tax-Deferred

Income or investment gains on which taxes are postponed until a later date.

Tax-Free

Income or investment gains that are not subject to taxation.

Time Horizon

The length of time an investor expects to hold an investment before needing the money.

Total Return

The overall gain or loss of an investment including price appreciation, dividends, and interest.

Traditional IRA

A retirement account that allows tax-deductible contributions and tax-deferred investment growth.

Bibliography

Bach, David. (2016). The Automatic Millionaire. Crown Business.

Bogle, John C. (2007). The Little Book of Common Sense Investing. Wiley.

Ramsey, Dave. (2013). The Total Money Makeover. Thomas Nelson.

Stanley/Danko. (1996). The Millionaire Next Door.

Kiyosaki, Robert. (2011). Rich Dad Poor Dad. Plata Publishing.

Robbins, Tony. (2014). MONEY: Master the Game. Simon & Schuster.

Fair Isaac Corporation. Understanding FICO Scores.

Consumer Financial Protection Bureau. Credit Reports and Scores.

U.S. Securities and Exchange Commission. Compound Interest Resources.

Berkshire Hathaway. Warren Buffett Shareholder Letters.

Your First 90-Day Unshackled Plan

Week 1 – Create your first intentional budget.

Week 2 – Pull your credit report.

Week 3 – List all debts and choose a payoff strategy.

Week 4 – Open or review your investment account.

Month 2 – Begin automatic investing.

Month 3 – Build or expand your emergency fund.

Progress is not built in a day. But disciplined action over 90 days can permanently change your financial trajectory.

About the Author

Stephen E. Kent is a motivational speaker, financial educator, former U.S. Army Colonel, former university CFO, and founder of Be the Best Foundation. His journey from poverty to financial freedom has made him a powerful voice on discipline, mindset, wealth building, and legacy.

Raised in the ghettos of Mississippi by a divorced mother surviving on welfare, food stamps, and faith, Kent often says he did not grow up poor. He grew up "PO." Determined to change the trajectory of his life, he earned a full academic scholarship and left for college after the 11th grade.

After 25 years in the active Army and serving at the rank of Colonel, Kent went on to serve as Vice President of Finance and CFO for multiple colleges in the Twin Cities metro area. But his financial journey was not without failure. Early in his military career, he found himself buried under $95,000 in credit card debt after chasing penny stocks and bad financial advice. Through discipline, education, investing, and long-term strategy, he rebuilt his life and eventually achieved a seven-figure net worth.

Today, Kent speaks to students, families, athletes, organizations, and underserved communities across the country about financial literacy, leadership, purpose, and generational wealth. Through his work with the Be the Best Foundation and the JustUs League and INsiders Mentoring Programs, he is committed to helping the next generation break financial cycles and build lives of freedom, impact, and significance.

StephenEKent.com
BetheBestFoundation.org

www.ingramcontent.com/pod-product-compliance
Lightning Source LLC
LaVergne TN
LVHW100318210926
848480LV00003B/1166
* 9 7 9 8 9 9 9 5 0 1 2 0 2 *